FJ

B.H. Brac

845388

Christmas 1991

HARVESTING
THE FIELD

HARVESTING
THE FIELD

An Anthology of Letters
From 1853 to the Present

Selected and Edited by
JAMES IRVINE ROBERTSON

Pelham Books

PELHAM BOOKS

Published by the Penguin Group
27 Wrights Lane, London W8 5TZ, England
Viking Penguin, a division of Penguin Books USA Inc
375 Hudson Street, New York, NY 10014, USA
Penguin Books Australia Ltd, Ringwood, Victoria, Australia
Penguin Books Canada Ltd, 10 Alcorn Avenue, Suite 300, Toronto, Ontario, Canada M4V 3B2
Penguin Books (NZ) Ltd, 182-190 Wairau Road, Auckland 10, New Zealand

Penguin Books Ltd, Registered Offices: Harmondsworth, Middlesex, England

First Published 1991
1 3 5 7 9 10 8 6 4 2

Typeset in 11/12 Goudy Old Style by Goodfellow & Egan Ltd, Cambridge.
Printed and bound in Great Britain by Butler & Tanner Ltd, Frome.

A CIP catalogue record for this book is available
from the British Library.

INTRODUCTION

IT IS NOT OFTEN EASY TO TOUCH the minds of past generations. Language, culture, the nature of belief change over the years and raise barriers of understanding. However, since *The Field* was founded in 1853 it is remarkable in many instances how little the concerns of its readers have changed. As vivid as ever are the observations made by readers on rural life and natural history and there is a bizarre topicality in their doubts on matters such as the feasibility of the Channel Tunnel and their disapproval of football hooligans.

The magazine was founded when the natural sciences were in their infancy and the land-owning gentry enthusiastically took up the challenge of explaining the habits of the denizens of the countryside, recording the changes they saw down the decades and submitting their observations and opinions to the scrutiny of the experts on *The Field* and the jury of their peers. The great country controversies were settled one by one. Woodcock do carry their young. Salmon do not eat in fresh water and their eggs are not eaten by dippers. Introducing alien animals into an environment can have unforeseen consequences. Mixed sex dormitories for farm servants are likely to encourage fornication.

It would have been possible, and probably sensible, to produce an anthology of great landmarks in the development of thinking on conservation and the countryside such as these, but this is not it. This is an anthology of quirks and eccentricities which is intended to shed some light on the attitudes and oddities as well as the achievements of the country dweller, human and otherwise, from the 1850s to the present day. This anthology concerns itself with matters like the incidence of passenger pigeons in Derbyshire, or ostriches swimming in the Mersey, of singing mice, of horses that murder sheep and the Duke of Wellington's breeches.

It is inconceivable that correspondents to *The Field* could ever have been profligate with the truth but, had they not always been gentlemen, some of their more curious observations might have made one inclined to wonder.

James Irvine Robertson, Dulverton 1991

1856

TEETOTAL HAYMAKING

SIR, I HAVE JUST entered on the fourth year of haymaking on teetotal principles. I have generally had four men to mow from 45 to 50 acres of grass and clover, and 12 to 16 men and boys haymaking. The mowers, I think, have each one quart of tea or coffee, milked and sugared, at 11 and 3 o'clock, in addition to which I paid them 6d. per acre extra instead of beer. The result has been most satisfactory both to myself and the men. Many, who at first declared it impossible to mow or reap without ale, have declared that they can do quite as well or better without, provided they have a good meal with some meat. These men have also said that they sleep much better after a hard day's work with tea etc., than with beer, and that they are much fresher and better able to begin again in the morning. There is, also, the absence of quarrelling, swearing, etc., so frequently the result of drinking in the hay and harvest field.

Yrs., JOSEPH TUCKER,
Bury Park, Beds.

UNSPORTSMANLIKE CONDUCT

SIR, I BEG PERMISSION, through your newspaper, to inform the gentlemen who hunt with Sir W. W. Wynn's hounds that a fox was trapped and killed on the night of Saturday the 18th or the morning of Sunday 19th instant, within two fields of my gorse-cover at Woodyate, by Samuel Brown, son of Charles Brown, gamekeeper at Loppington. I think it right to make the fact publicly known, because, though a fellow cannot be legally punished for destroying a fox on land in his own occupation, he will, upon his vulpicidal propensity being made known, deservedly become a *marked man* in the district in which he may reside.

Yrs., ROBERT CHAMBRE VAUGHAN,
Burlton Hall, nr. Shrewsbury

BREEDING

SIR, A MARE BELONGING to the late Sir Gore Ouseley had a foal by a quagga, which was, as might be expected, marked with the stripes and colours of its sire. Three years afterwards the mare had a foal by a thoroughbred horse, which had similar markings, but not so clearly expressed. A medical case is recorded, too, of a lady having a coloured child under circumstances which by no possibility could bring any shadow of imputation against her, and which extraordinary fact could only be accounted for by reason of her imagination having been influenced by a portrait of an Oriental which hung opposite her bed, and to which portrait the child bore a strong resemblance.

Yrs., 'CIRCUMNAVIGATION'

DEFENCE AGAINST BURGLARS

SIR, I CONSIDER COLT'S repeating pistol the very best defence of all, the 5 in. barrel is the most handy. The next best description of weapon is the old-fashioned rapier or small sword; and I know not a handier weapon for defence or attack and it is a weapon that those ruffians have not the least idea how to defend themselves against.

The ordinary navy cutlass is a most formidable weapon in the hands of a powerful man and this is the best weapon wherewith to arm servants who may not be accustomed to firearms.

Yrs., J.W.J.

1858

REARING GROUSE

Sir, In a small town to the west of this about 18 miles, there lived a shoemaker on the ground floor of a thatched cottage; in his garret (which had a window in the gable) he placed on the floor a quantity of gravel, earth, and sand, large sods of heather, as he was close to the moor, rushes, ferns and everything he could fancy grouse fed or loved to sit amongst: there he placed a pair of tame grouse, and they bred the same as on the moor. They fed on corn and heather, and were lovely birds, tame and confiding. 'Cock, cock' 'Go back! Go back!' resounded from the shoemaker's loft; and the gor-cock was there in his pride and beauty (the blessed bird!) as if on his native hill. Birds of this description are frequently offered to me for sale; and I will be most happy to aid any gentleman in procuring a brace or two to breed from, should they express the wish to have them.

Yrs., D.F.P.,
Edinburgh

SALMON IN TEES

Sir, I amused myself for a whole afternoon watching the salmon leap at Dinsdale Lock, on the Tees, 6 miles above Yarm, wantonly shooting at them with a bullet. I saw vast numbers of fish jump from 4 to 5 ft. in height against the falling water, two or three fish often being out of the water at a time. These fish invariably fell back again, the height of their springs never reaching above one third of the height of the fall. Yet I saw more than a score of fish go over. These fish *swam* up the perpendicular falls of water without starting with any jump, at an angle of from 30° to 45°. Every fish that took the diagonal course seemed to succeed, resting on the top, close to the edge of the fall, recovering their 'wind'.

Yrs., 'PILGRIM'

CAT NUISANCE

SIR, A CORRESPONDENT OF yours writes to know how he can get rid of cats. I cannot tell him how to get rid of them; but I can tell him how to collect around him all the cats in the neighbourhood – viz, buying 6d. worth of the herb valerian at any druggists and, after putting as much as he can take up between his finger and thumb in some boiling water, throw it out anywhere – if he likes, over a trap lightly covered (or half a dozen traps, if he prefers it) – and he will have troops of cats assembling every night around the magic herb. The best plan is to get a large slab of iron hung about 2 ft. over the ground, which might be freed easily by a jerk of the string which fastens it. Under this put the valerian, and kill five or six cats at a time – as shown in the accompanying sketch.

Yrs., 'ANTI CATTITE'

[What will the pro-cattites have to say to this? – Ed.]

SALMON IN TWEED

SIR, ON SUNDAY, 22 August, I saw such a run of fish as I never saw surpassed, and hardly equalled. I went to the river at about 11 o'clock in the forenoon and, with the exception of half an hour for dinner, I was there till 3 o'clock p.m., and I have no doubt but that 3,000 or 4,000 fish passed upwards in that time, a great proportion of them being heavy salmon. I have fished at Tweedmill all my time, and I never saw such a sight but once, many years ago.

Yrs., JOHN SCOTT,
Tweedmill, Coldstream

BIRDS OF PASSAGE

SIR, IN THE WINTER OF 1847, weather hard, with deep snow, an enormous flight of migratory birds took place; it consisted chiefly of larks and linnets, but there were also a few blackbirds and thrushes, with fieldfares, redwings and furze chats. Having observed that the larks were inclined to pitch on any spot clear of snow, I swept a space of about 10 yds. in length by about 4 ft. broad at either end of my lawn, and threw down some cabbage leaves and a few oats. The larks pitched there eagerly, and it was as much as I could do to fire and load, pick up and change places fast enough to receive them as they came. In the first two days I bagged 552 larks, 13 fieldfares and 35 redwings. I could have killed thousands more. On the whole line of flight, 2 or 3 miles inland, enormous damage was done by the larks, and whole turnip fields divested of every atom of green leaf.

Yrs., GRANTLEY F. BERKELEY

DEGENERACY OF THOROUGHBREDS

SIR, THERE CAN BE NO doubt our English thoroughbred is a degenerate animal. We sometimes hear his speed mentioned as an argument on the opposite side, and it is possible that Priam or Bay Middleton might have beaten Eclipse or Childers, and that the stop watches of our great-grandfathers are not to be implicitly believed in. There may be a few flyers, and a few really useful horses, but what are the mass but useless, weedy, spindle-shanked rips? Let anyone who doubts it go to Tattersall's and peep into the boxes. The great misfortune is that these racing blood cast-offs are the sires of most of our hunters, etc. Different kinds of unsoundness and weakness commonly go together; thus the animal with small legs has also a small waist, and is lame and a roarer also. There was a horse called Autocrat at Tattersall's last week, belonging to a gentleman deceased. Well, he comes from a racing family, is a son of Bay Middleton, and may get some race horse, but think you such legs and feet will get a sound and useful horse? His ankles were like an antelope's. Where are we to look for means of improvement? Not to any Arab I have ever seen. They have not the weight, length, and strength which we require. I have seen a fair number of Arab crosses and they are more useless (if possible) than the non-racing racer. The main suggestion that occurs to me is, eschew the '16 hands and upwards'. It is those tall animals that are lame and roarers; but do not go for the 14-hands Arab, he is too small and light, but take pains to find a horse that is, and always has been, sound – that is as near 15.2 as you can get him, with as much bone as may be, and standing on much ground.

Yrs., 'Q. IN THE CORNER'

1859

RECREATIONS FOR THE CLERGY

SIR, TO ME TOP BOOTS peering under a surplice are no attraction, nor do I particularly admire the hunter-in-waiting at the church door. In fact, I am unable to discover the peculiar ability to show me the way to Heaven of the man who is pursuing worldly amusements during the week and mounting the pulpit on Sundays. The dull multitude like myself, who read plain simple English with a plain simple comprehension, see a sporting clergyman out of place and disregarding the most sacred of obligations.

Yrs., 'T'

THE GRAND NATIONAL

SIR, IN NOTICING the above affair last week, I regret that you were not a little more energetic in your condemnation of so gross a piece of folly and absurdity. Grand indeed! Time was when the term might have applied with propriety in the early days of steeplechasing – when the horses carried from 11 to 12 stone each over a stiff hunting country. But in the present case, when a lot of old cast-off racers are to carry 8 or 9 stone over a course that a donkey might cross, it is something more than ridiculous. Why, the man who made this handicap could know nothing of hunting or hunters, or he would not have put it on the footing of a rascally racing handicap. If a horse cannot carry 11 or 12 stone, he ought not to be called a hunter or entered as such.

The fact is that steeplechasing in this country has descended into the hands of the racing and gambling fraternity, and become nothing more or less than a clumsy cobweb, by which they catch and suck the foolish flies who buzz about our racecourses. Hunting men and breeders of hunters have cut the concern in disgust; and it must soon have an end, and it cannot be too soon.

Yrs., 'OBSERVATOR'

STEAM-ENGINES ON TURNPIKE ROADS

SIR, ARE YOU AWARE THAT there is a Bill before Parliament for regulating the use of locomotives on turnpike and other roads? If this is passed, it will be almost impossible for anyone, more especially ladies, to ride or drive along such roads.

Mr McAdam says that horses will in the course of time get accustomed to them. But I should like to know how many lives would be lost in that 'course' of 'accustoming'?

Stop the Bill, or turnpike roads and highways will be useless to those that prefer horseflesh to steam.

Yrs., JOHN PLEYDELL,
London

1860

POSTAGE STAMPS

SIR, SEVERAL LADIES OF my acquaintance are collecting spent postage stamps. Can anyone inform me what it is for, as I have heard various accounts?

Yrs., 'INQUIRER'

[Many of those collected are not used in a legitimate manner, but are fraudulently made to look as new, and sold again at a low price. – Ed.]

TOURIST *v* TRAVELLER

THE QUESTION 'WHAT IS a tourist?' is as difficult of solution as the celebrated enigma 'What is a pound?' It has been stated what extraordinary powers of observation and judgement are required to make a traveller; but quite another order of qualities go to the making up of the tourist. In the first place he must be entirely destitute of any powers of observation or of adapting himself to the manners of the people among whom he moves. He must have no object in his tour but to pass the time and idle about and he 'sees' things and 'does' things merely that he may go home and say that he has 'seen' and 'done' them. The idea of seeking by travel to increase his knowledge never enters his head. He carries his habits, his prejudices, sometimes even his acquaintances and his family with him as a snail carries his house upon his back. He tests everything he meets by comparison with these and condemns whatever is new in proportion as it differs from them.

1861

EPISODE IN THE HUNTING FIELD

SIR, ON TUESDAY, the North Warwickshire Hounds met at the Bull at Weston and, towards the close of the run, an incident occurred which is happily rare in the hunting field. One of the members of the hunt attempted to cross the private garden of a farmer whilst the huntsman was making his cast. The good lady of the house having allowed the huntsmen to enter to do their business, the farmer politely requested 'the gentleman' not to enter his garden and plough it up. This remonstrance was ineffectual, the person addressed was evidently incapable of perceiving what was 'the right thing' to do and, after a few words had passed, struck the farmer on the head. The latter returned the blow and challenged his assailant to get off his horse to do battle royal in the good old English style. This request was not acceded to, but Reynard, having made a ring, the field again came in the same direction and the farmer mounted his steed and, as the hounds were coming across his own grounds, rode up to and asked the 'gentleman' in pink if he was the person who had previously struck him.

Being answered in the affirmative, he then proceeded to bestow a most severe flagellation, obliging the gentleman to dismount and John Bull actually whipped this fashionable fox hunter with no sparing hand until he was off his land. The offender, meanwhile, showing the white feather disgracefully, the field cried 'shame' that one of their order should be guilty of such conduct and applauded the straightforward and plucky conduct of the farmer. They also insisted that the 'gentleman' should apologise and the offence was, I am happy to say, forgiven by the bold yeoman to whom an apology was not only offered but a very handsome testimonial also presented by the apologiser. You will be surprised to learn the ages of the actors in this scene. The farmer is over 50 years and a very heavy weight. The 'gentleman' about 25 and 6 feet in height.

Were the conduct of this person to be generally imitated and private grounds invaded thus, fox hunting would soon cease to be the popular sport it now is.

Yrs., 'ONE WHO SAW IT ALL'

RAILWAY PARROTS

SIR, AT ALMOST EVERY station between Edinburgh and Glasgow, the station master has a starling or parrot so trained that whenever a train draws up at the platform it commences calling out the name of the station most distinctly and continues to scream it out until the train starts. This is found to be an economical mode of informing passengers where they are and as this is the season for securing young starlings, I would recommend you to make the matter public through the columns of your paper.

Yrs., 'BUILDER'

[We willingly do so but suggest nevertheless that until the starlings are trained, railway porters be compelled to speak distinctly. – Ed.]

FROTHY CREAM

SIR, MY MASTER TAKES in *The Field* and I oftentime gets a peep in it. Why do you call it *The Field?* I never saw anything green in it. Fields are always green in these parts excepting when we have snow or white frost as it is now. However I suppose you know best about that. As for me I have always found it a garden for I have gathered lots of fruit out of it and now my troubling you with this is to get more.

Will you or some of your good-natured ladies and gentlemen (they always appear to be telling you something) tell me what I wants to know which is why my cream (I mean my master's cows' cream) lately froths up in the churn and will not come to butter? I have warmed the cream and almost churned my heart out but no butter comes. I have then put the churn and cream in cold water for hours but still no butter comes and it is still frothy and for the life of me I cannot get any butter. Now do, good Mr Editor, get me, if you can, the reason why this is and what will be still better, how I can get butter from my churn full of frothy cream now in the dairy. Missus thinks it's my fault. I know, although she doesn't say so. I see she doesn't like to be deprived of her nice fresh butter. Neither do I, if it comes to that. Therefore do, good Mr Editor, get me the information and I shall be ever grateful.

Yrs., 'SARRATT DAIRYMAID'

ROMAN OATS

IN A FIELD OF THE farm occupied by Mr Binks, at Peppermoor, near Alnwick, some ancient encampments long existed which tradition ascribed to the Romans. The

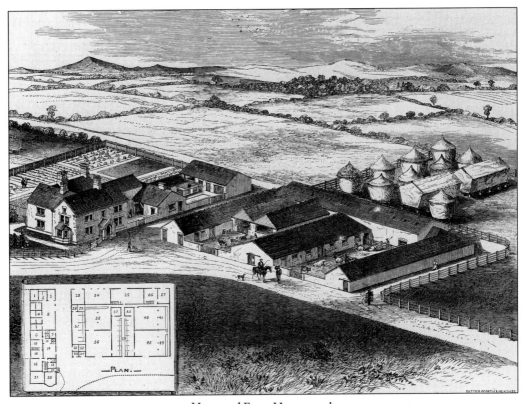

Haywood Farm Homestead

lapse of time and the spirit of agricultural improvement gradually obliterated almost every trace of them, and about a year ago the last of the whins which time out of mind had covered the ground where the Roman legionaries had trodden were cut down and the land sown with barley. When the barley was ready for the sickle, Mr Binks was astonished to observe several heads of strange-looking oats amongst it. Some of them were unusually tall and strong, with long branching stemlets, whilst others had globular heads resem-

bling the seed of the onion. Mr Binks collected no less than 75 varieties never seen in the district before. He has sown the seed, and intends to exhibit a collection of them at the next show of the Alnwick Horticultural Society. The place, it has been conjectured, has been a cavalry camp; and the oats, which were perhaps ripened under other skies, after lying covered with the debris of the camp for fifteen hundred years, will again shoot into cereal beauty, and may add one or more permanent varieties to the stock of the English farmer.

1862

ANTI-GAROTTE GLOVE

SIR, I HAVE BEEN REQUESTED to examine an ingenious contrivance which has been brought out partly by a medical man and partly by the inventor as an instantaneous defence against the garotte attacks which are now so frequent in our streets. The invention consists of a pair of very strong leather gloves which, from their appearance, would not give any idea of the wearer having about him weapons of defence. Upon the inside of the last phalanx or joint of the thumb and of the middle finger are firmly fastened with an extra bit of leather a pair of sharp cutting powerful steel curved claws, the insides of which are sharpened to a knife edge. The glove is made very strong expressly to withstand a struggle and is held firm by an ingenious fastening at the wrist.

The mode of action is this: the garotter pounces upon his victim from behind a doorway or other hiding place and throws his arm round the neck; the immediate and natural instinct of the *garottee* is to throw up his hands and pull at the entwining arm. The steel claws of the glove immediately penetrate the clothes and not only wound but also cut at the same time. The pain thus caused will compel the garotter to release his hold immediately.

Yrs., FRANK T. BUCKLAND

A WORD FOR THE CABMAN

SIR, IT APPEARS TO BE the fashion now to abuse and vilify the poor cabby. Very few people know anything of the condition or circumstances of the cabman; they expect him to be at their beck any hour of the day or night, to take them anywhere at 6d. per mile, the liberal price fixed by an enlightened legislature, particularly for the accommodation of MPs who require to be driven from the House of Commons to Pall Mall for 6d. Not above two per cent of London cabs belong to the persons driving them, the remainder are hired out per day, including the use of two horses, at prices varying, according to the season, from 12s. to 24s. The cabman's expenses generally amount to about 3s. per day. He is out from 16 to 18 hours, and is obliged to get his meals at public houses or cook shops wherever he happens to be. Thirty miles is the average number of miles each horse is driven in order to get together the master's money and, consequently, the mortality amongst the horses is very great.

Yrs., M.M.

SHOOTING IN ALBANIA

SIR, WOODCOCK, WILD DUCK, snipe, jackal and wild boar are to be found there. Live at Corfu; a small yacht is indispensable. Butrinto and Catilo are the best landing-places. Not an ounce of decent powder is to be had on Corfu. Get a letter of credit on Taylor of Corfu (a correspondent of Messrs Glyn, Mills and Co.), who is a general agent, and provides everything and everybody. Take a good hunting whip in lieu of an ordinary dog whip, as shepherd dogs are most annoying and cowardly, but know the range of ordinary dog whips.

Yrs., M.A.C.

LARGE TROUT

SIR, ON THE FIRST OF September I went out as usual pike fishing on Lough Dearg with my otter board, which carries nine baits, spoons, etc. It was blazing hot at the time, as bright a sun as we have had all year, and quite calm. When I got a fierce pull at a spoon, next the otter, I said it was a pike and commenced to play him cautiously. I should have said that when I hooked the fish, it at once pulled the otter under water, and ran with it ahead of the cot. It soon came up but to go down again, and sometimes my rowers had to pull their best after him. In about 10 minutes, as the fish had not showed, I said it must be a salmon – a big pike always shows after a bit; at length, after about 40 minutes or more, I caught a sight of the fish, stationary with his great fins at work, about 3 ft. down in the water, when I made a chance stroke of the gaff at him, striking him in the middle of the back, balancing him as nicely as possible. The fish then struggled like a porpoise, and, failing to bring him in with one hand, I let go the other line and lugged him over the boat's side; then, to my amazement, I found it was a splendid trout. My boatman shouted for joy for 5 minutes. The trout weighed 29 lb. 6 oz. He was seen by a number of Englishmen here for the fishing, and by E. F. Ryan, Esq, R.M., who took a sketch of the fish. He was 3 ft. 7 in.

long and 2 ft. in girth, and his splendid condition surprised all who saw him. He was truly one of the great Irish lake trout.

Yrs., JNO W. PEPPER,
S.I. Constabulary, Mount
Shannon, Scarriff, Co. Galway

SLAVERY

SIR, AS THE COLUMNS OF *The Field* are open to the chase in all its branches, I shall describe a species of sport which, if once commenced, is, I believe, the most absorbing and surpasses all others in interest – this is 'Man-hunting', a recreation that converts a human being into a demon; that entirely eradicates every germ of goodness that nature may have planted within him, and that brings a curse upon a country which induces a moral waste far more blightful than Africa's widest desert.

The slave-trade of the White Nile has, within the last three years, increased to the present maximum. It is conducted upon two systems: the one, an open act of piracy; the other, a combination of commerce with robbery and murder. The former is a simple armament fitted out at Khartoum, comprising sundry sailing vessels, with a party from 60 to 250 armed men; these sail up the White Nile in November, and, landing at various points, they attack and burn the village, shoot the men, and capture the women and children. The captives are then pinioned, their necks being secured on a long cleft-pole, to which their wrists are bound as though in handcuffs and are thus driven in long strings to the slavers' boats.

The required number of slaves being secured, they are crowded in the boats for transport to the market in such numbers that sickness is frequently induced by filth and close contact; in such cases the sufferers are thrown overboard, helpless children are flung into the river to drown; young girls, who have first ministered to the lusts of their captors, are mercilessly given to the Nile. *The crocodile is the sexton of the White Nile.* Frequently the entire cargo of slaves thus perishes by an epidemic: and the remedy? – a fresh raid.

The commercial system of the White Nile is at least quaint and original. The tribes, having learnt the demand for ivory, will not exchange for beads as formerly; they require cattle, and will take nothing else in barter. The trader accordingly starts with an armed expedition, like his brother pirate, and, attacking the first village, he captures all the cattle. Having plundered a succession of weak tribes and secured some hundred or thousand cattle, he drives them into ivory country and exchanges them for elephants' tusks. Having exhausted his stock, he is hard up for capital; without bullocks there can be no business. He accordingly allies himself with a tribe hostile to his recent purchasers, with the intention of attacking them and stealing back all the beasts he has exchanged.

At that heavy hour just before the first grey streak of dawn pierces the darkness, when most men sleep their soundest, the trader's party surrounds the village of his late customers – the straw huts are fired. Before the victims are awake, the crackling of flames breaks upon their dreams – a volley of musketry rattles among the affrighted fugitives, as panic-stricken they strive to escape through smoke and fire; they are helplessly shot down. The young women and children are captured, together with the whole of the cattle recently exchanged; the latter at this early hour being conveniently situated in the village 'Zarceba', or thorn enclosure.

The animals are now shared with the allies, the trader taking half. With these he barters with his new friends for ivory, which he sends to his boats. He once more has the advantage of knowing where his cattle are; he therefore seeks the alliance of another tribe, and attacks the recent cattle purchasers, not only recapturing his bullocks, but shooting his late friends, and kidnapping the women and children without mercy. Thus the same animals produce an immense supply of ivory as they are bartered and restolen several times.

The trader is too much for the unsophisticated savages, whose individual jealousies he turns to his own interest. He at length arrives with his productive cattle among a tribe too powerful to insult; he therefore honestly barters his beasts for ivory, and returns to his boats laden with tusks and slaves. The latter, of course, undergo all the miseries already described. It will naturally be asked, 'Who are these White Nile slave traders?' Turks, Syrians, Arabs, and *Europeans* are engaged in this atrocious piracy; and the British flag, instead of being known to the negroes as the emblem of freedom, frequently covers a slave cargo. In this wretched country, where the wild beast prowls by night throughout the land, and the crocodile awaits you in every stream, there is no enemy so great to man as man himself; no beast, however savage, so bloodthirsty as his own kind.

Yrs., SAMUEL W. BAKER

1863

RED BEARDS AND DEFECTIVE VISION

SIR, I READ A LETTER SOME time ago in your paper remarking on a peculiarity in the organs of hearing in white cats with blue eyes. I should feel obliged by your giving me your opinion on a somewhat similar phenomenon which has always puzzled me. It is this: Why gentlemen with red beards are generally apparently afflicted with defective vision? I cannot account in any other way for the rude stares one receives from gentlemen 'in red'. I counted no less than thirty of these unfortunate cases in the park the other day; and I assure you the way almost all of them stared was such as to make one feel quite uncomfortable. A dark or fair man will walk on pretending he has not observed you; or, if he does raise his eyes to look at you, he will do so in a quiet, unobtrusive way; but a man with a red beard will invariably give a bold stare, half stop as though going to speak, and stand looking after you when you have passed on. Now, sir, I cannot attribute this to any-thing but some peculiarity in the eyesight. If quadrupeds with blue eyes are frequently deaf, why should not bipeds with red beards be troubled with a near-sightedness which renders them seemingly imperti-nent? I hope that you will be able to throw some light on this interesting question.

Yrs., 'A VICTIM'

Her Majesty's pet dog 'Looty'

Sir, Your lovely correspondent, 'A Victim' appears to be annoyed at being stared at by gentlemen in 'red' and further states that 'he stands looking after you when you have passed on'. Now it is quite apparent that the lovely 'Victim' must turn round to look after the gentlemen in 'red', otherwise it would be impossible to know that he was looking after her when she had passed on. Deaf white cats, with blue eyes, may look at kings, and the lovely 'Victim' must allow us in 'red' to look at her.

Yrs., 'ONE IN RED'

SALMON ANGLING ON TWEED

SIR, ON THE WHOLE THE season has been a most successful one on the middle waters. Fish have been very abundant, and have generally been of large size and in beautiful condition. The visit of H.R.H. Prince Alfred to the Tweed was amply sufficient of itself to mark out the angling season of 1863; and it was a source of general pleasure that in the course of the few hours during which he plied the water he succeeded in killing no fewer than five fine fish, one of which weighed 23 lb. The heaviest day's take fell to the rod of the Duke of Roxburghe, who captured 15 fish, all heavy weights. Mr Dennistoun killed 12, the Master of Lovat 11, Mr Tyler 11, the Marquis of Bowmont 12. Lord Dunglass, the Earl of Tankerville, the Hon Harry Grey, Mr Prescott, Sir George Douglas, Lord Charles Ker, Lord W. Thynne, Dr Geldart, the Hon Mr Barrington, Lord Llanover, Mr George H. Thompson etc., had all capital sport. The largest fish which has been landed in the season weighed 41 lb., and was killed by Sir John Lees in the Cornhill water. Another splendid fish, weighing 35 lb., was killed by the Master of Lovat on the Floors water. Of runs, there were two very remarkable, one in which a salmon weighing 20 lb., hooked by Mr Dennistoun, ran over the Kelso cauld; the skilful angler, got on the bank, managed to pass the cauld ere the fish had run out of reach, and, after an exciting struggle, succeeded, much to the surprise of the lookers on, in landing it; such an incident, perhaps, never occurred on the Tweed before. The other run referred to Mr Walter Mathieson, who, after running a fish of 24½ lb. for 4½ hours over difficult and dangerous ground, succeeded in landing it an hour after dark. Lord Gardner, in 55 days, killed 299 fish, weighing in the aggregate 3,792 lb. The avidity with which the sport of salmon-angling is now sought after is very great, and seems yearly to be on the increase.

Yrs., ANCRAM

MARE'S NEST

SIR, MY GROOM, ON visiting the stable this morning, was surprised to see that the tail of my mare had undergone, during the night, a most extraordinary entanglement; and was even more astonished to find that a fine, fat mouse, *enceinte*, had made a most cosy nest there, no doubt, as a careful mother mouse would, with a view to introducing some half a dozen young dependents on my corn bin.

Yrs., 'GRATEFUL'

1864

HOW TO MAKE THE DONKEY GO

SIR, A FRIEND IS ABOUT to take out a patent for the following ingenious mode of driving a donkey. He writes to me as follows:- 'Whilst walking through the market place of Knaresborough a few days ago, I observed my milkman driving his donkey cart. I inquired of him whether he was going to the sale at Scotton (2 miles off). He replied he was; so I asked him if there was room for another to ride in the cart, he answered there was; and I (not having anything particular to do) thought I would have a ride behind the moke. So up I got, and away we went at a tolerable speed, he using the whip pretty freely until we got out of town; then he observed "I will show you how he can go." With that he put his hand into his coat pocket and drew out from thence a large bullock's bladder, containing a few peas; but as soon as he began to blow into it, the "Fuzzack" pricked up his ears (and I can assure you he was not without these ornaments, being a cross from the Spanish tribe), and off we went, helter-skelter, doing the distance of over two miles in a quarter of an hour. I never was in the company of a more lively donkey in my life, so I should recommend this mode of donkey-driving to all persons who are inclined to use those useful animals.' This reminds me of the story of the lady who used to drive a pair of donkeys, which were wonderful goers. Her secret was not found out for some time, when an inquiring mind ascertained that there was a sharp pin concealed in the tassel at the end of her parasol, with which she used to *encourage* her steeds.

Yrs., FRANK T. BUCKLAND

DESTRUCTION OF KINGFISHERS

SIR, THE NATURALIST READERS of *The Field* will hear with regret of the wholesale destruction which is now going on of our elegant little kingfisher; no less than thirty of these birds having been killed and supplied to a fashionable millinery and hat-makers (as I was credibly informed by the proprietress) in a very short space of time, for the purpose of embellishing ladies' hats, notwithstanding the price given for each bird is very trivial. It is to be hoped that some of the writers in *The Field* will protest against this attempt at annihilation, as the kingfisher is at present scarce enough, being rarely or ever seen in many districts; otherwise total extirpation may be the result.

Yrs., EDWIN WARD,
Manchester-square

PORPOISE IN THAMES

SIR, ON THURSDAY MORNING, the 21st April, at about 8 o'clock, a porpoise was observed in the Thames near the ferry at Isleworth. Two boatmen succeeded in driving it into shallow water, where they killed it by breaking in the skull with a crowbar. The animal proved to be a female with young; the foetus was nearly (or quite) full-grown, about 18 in. long. The barbarity of the captors is only excusable on the grounds of extreme ignorance; the fellows, appearing highly elated by the achievement, placed it on a hand-barrow and carried it through the streets of Richmond, collecting coppers by the exhibition. It is stated that about ten years since a porpoise was taken nearly in the same part of the river, and met the same fate. It is difficult to imagine what induced the creature to swim a distance of nearly 30 miles in fresh water, unless, having been alarmed at the mouth of the river, and prompted by the maternal

Group of some of the members of the Thames Angling Society

[26]

instinct, she sought safety in flight. It must be regretted that so interesting a specimen of marine mammalia should have been so cruelly destroyed. I have requested the boatmen of the neighbourhood to keep a sharp look-out, and should they have a chance of catching another porpoise to preserve it alive, and immediately to communicate with the Editor of *The Field*, who I doubt not would gladly avail himself of such a prize.

Yrs., R. GOODWIN MURRAY

[It is a grievous pity that such an excellent opportunity of enriching the collection at the Zoological Gardens with such an interesting specimen – and one likely from its presence in fresh water, to be easily naturalised in some of the tanks – should have been lost through the ignorance of the captors. We remember seeing the former porpoise at Isleworth. It was carried about Richmond for coppers after the same manner as the present one has been. It was a fine specimen, nearly 5 ft. in length. – Ed.]

NOVEL METHOD OF CROSS FISHING

SIR, TWO POOR PEASANT boys in this neighbourhood, without the assistance of rods, wheels, or otter, have been very successful cross fishers. They merely hold either ends of a line, which is about 10 yds. longer than the breadth of a narrow river, using 3 or 4 ft. of gut suspended by a swivel from its centre, and but one hook baited with a natural fly, which they immediately drop over any fish which may rise within view. Should they happen to hook a large trout, they play him by running towards the banks, and retiring from them whenever the line becomes slack. I suspect they were not able to procure rods, but their excuse was that the shadow of the rods scared the fish on a calm day. Truly 'necessity is the mother of invention'.

Yrs., 'A GOOD OBSERVER',
Roscrea

[The poaching young scamps ought to have been well whipped. – Ed.]

A DEVOTED DOG AND CONSTANT MOURNER

SIR, MANY PEOPLE ADMIT and acknowledge the affection of the dog, and yet know not half its love. Five years ago a dog, a cross of the terrier breed, followed its master's funeral to the Old Grey Friars' church-yard, in this city; it saw all it loved on earth laid in the grave, and there poor Bob has remained ever since. He is fed plentifully by the kind-hearted neighbours, takes walks with any friend to the end of the next street, bids him good bye, and returns to his home in the church-yard. Here is love surpassing all that of other animals! How cruel a thing it is to ill use the dog, man's truest and most steadfast friend! How thoughtless to rend the ties by exchanging and parting with your favourite, just to get one you think looks better! This love and affection is confined to no particular breed at all. I have every opportunity to study their character, as I am superintendent of the Home for Lost Dogs in Edinburgh, and have there all kinds.

Yrs., D.P.F.,
Edinburgh

1865

CLASS WILL OUT

ENGLISH GENTLEMEN FEEL A very great sympathy with their peers in most things. Above all, perhaps, in their superiority to men of a lower class of society in their capability for athletic sports. There can be no doubt that in any competition of this kind between the gentlemen of the country and an equal number of the middle classes, the gentlemen would prove victorious. Not only is it notorious as a fact, but it stands to reason that it must ever remain so, that for general hardihood, courage, activity and that manual dexterity which is more an instinct than a requirement, high breeding and association are the best instructors.

POLLUTION OF RICKMANSWORTH FISHERY. VERDICT AGAINST PAPER MAKER

SIR, THERE HAVE BEEN FEW cases of greater interest to the large body of anglers than this case. The defendant is a man of mark, owning several paper mills in different parts of the country. Costs to the extent of £2,000 is not such a flea bite and the person damaged has the satisfaction of knowing that his opponent has to pay pretty smartly for his whistle and will not be likely in the face of such a verdict to indulge in that very expensive process in paper making involved in the use of esparto and the turning of the refuse into a trout fishery. This case, it is to be hoped, will not only serve as a warning to paper makers all over the country as showing them how, by the reckless use of their chemicals, they may be put to some £2,000 costs beyond their calculations, but will also put the owners of waters which are damaged by such processes on the *qui vive* to take up the cudgels and proceed against the destroyers of their property. It cannot be doubted after such a sharp lesson as the above that paper makers will be inclined to examine a little more closely and patiently into the plans and propositions for tanks and filtering apparatus which are easily applicable and at comparatively small cost to all paper works.

Yrs., FRANCIS FRANCIS

FIRST FIELD TRIAL OF POINTERS AND SETTERS

THIS MUCH ANTICIPATED trial took place on Tuesday on the manor of Southill, Bedfordshire, the property of S. Whitbread, Esq, MP, and everything passed off as satisfactorily as circumstances would permit. The ground is exceedingly well adapted for the purpose, the fields being large, a great part of the land being wheat, and birds and hares in large numbers. Notwithstanding what has been said about the delay in bringing off the trial, it would have been advantageous if it could have taken place even a fortnight later, as owing to the backwardness of the season, the young wheat and clover did not afford such good cover as they would have done in ordinary years. The day was not a good scenting one, being close and hot, and with scarcely a breath of air. The pointers were first tested, so as to give the setters the opportunity of being run at a cooler part of the day; but 'the best laid plans of mice and men gang aft agley,' and the fickle weather changed to its hottest at the period devoted to the longer-haired animals. The dogs on the whole acquitted themselves very well – some brilliantly; *escapades* were few and far between; but it is not for us to go into particulars – they must be left for the official announcement at the time of the exhibition. Mr Bailey, steward to Mr Whitbread, was unremitting in his endeavours to afford the utmost facility for fair testing the dogs; and by placing horses at the disposal of the judges, he enabled those gentlemen to perform their duties, not only with greater ease to themselves, but with a precision which could not have been

Prize dogs at the North of England Show, Islington

attained had they been on foot. The judges wish us to express their strong sense of his kindness and courtesy, and also to acknowledge the zealous attentions of Mr Thompson, the head keeper. We are sure we are only expressing the wishes of sportsmen in general in thanking Mr Whitbread for the almost unsurpassable advantages he has afforded for carrying out this novel undertaking; and we hope, through his kindness, to have to report on a similar trial, on a still larger scale, in another year.

WINE SALE

RECENTLY WAS HELD A remarkable sale of wine in Carlisle, which had been the property of the late Mr George Blamire, barrister-at-law. The stock was not large, but it comprised samples of some of the finest vintages known. To quote the words of the auctioneer, in the catalogue: 'The ports of 1820, imported and supplied in 1822, by Harris, Crutchedfriars, London, have all the characteristics of that wonderful vintage; the charming violet bouquet of the splendid comet wine of 1811 is here in all its richness and perfection: while the crisp and dry sherries, the elegant, nectar-like Madeiras, the luscious lachryma, and the pure sans-dated ports of the last century, are all invested with an ineffable delicacy that can only be acquired in the etherialising laboratory of Nature'. Agents from all parts of the kingdom attended to compete for these treasures and both the competition and prices were (we may safely say) unprecedented. One lot of six dozen of the finest and most perfect 1820 port was purchased at £35 the dozen for a Yorkshire

ironmaster; other lots sold at £27, £17, £13 10s., £13, £10 10s., the dozen. The highest prices fetched by Madeira were £10, £9 10s.

1866

BEE SWARM SETTLING ON THE FACE

SIR, IN JUNE, 1854, Mr James Simmonds, a farmer, residing at Brooklands Farm, Weybridge, and a tenant of the Hon. Locke King, MP, was dressing in order to attend the rent audit at Woburn House. Before putting on his coat he perceived from his window an unusually large swarm of bees filling the air with their cloud and noise. It was, in fact, two swarms that had come from two distinct hives and united in the air. He ran out in his shirt sleeves and without a hat, to see where they would alight. The bees, after making some circles in the air, led him to the banks of the river Wey, to within 50 yards of the spot called the Seven Arches. Thinking that the bees might cross the river and escape, he adopted a plan not uncommon with beemasters, that of throwing dust into the air among the bees. This often makes them settle quickly. They did settle quickly, and this more so than he expected, for in a short time the whole of one of the largest swarms he had ever seen settled on his head, face and breast. They hung down in front like a great beard to the bottom of his waistcoat. Had he not been well accustomed to bees, and perfectly collected, his situation would have been a very dangerous one; for had he at all irritated this mass of armed insects, he would have no doubt received a sufficient number of stings to place his life in peril. He was obliged to close his eyes slowly and keep his mouth shut. Then, in order to prevent their entering his nostrils, which they endeavoured to do, he slowly thrust one hand through the mass, and with two fingers managed to keep pushing and drawing them away from his nostrils as they tried to enter, he breathing all the while as softly as possible. His first thought was to walk slowly into the river, but every little agitation, however slight, caused a hum and a hiss from some thousands. Mr Simmonds slowly knelt down on his knees and remained perfectly still. He then found that bees were beginning to gather in a mass below the waistband of his trousers, indicating that the queen was there. Fearing that the tightness of the waistband – rendered tighter whenever he breathed – might crush or irritate this part of the swarm, he slowly unbuttoned the front of his trousers.

At this moment he heard a railway train on the Chertsey Branch Railway, from which he was about 50 yards. It fortunately happened that the engine-driver was known to him and had a little commission from him to sound his railway whistle if he saw anything wrong among his cows or sheep. Seeing Mr Simmonds on his knees, with one arm extended as if for help and something odd on his face, the driver sounded his whistle. This was heard by Mrs Simmonds who sent her son and a farming man out into the fields and they found Mr Simmonds in the predicament described. In addition to the hanging mass there was a

'The Aerial Chair'

[33]

cloud of bees still flying round him, so to approach him was not the most agreeable office. However they came near enough to hear him speak, which he did very gently, merely saying 'Bring a bushel hive, well rubbed with honey, and some bricks'.

While they were gone at top speed for these, he remained perfectly still. The tickling of the bees' feet on his face was almost unbearable, and the danger of irritating those that were down his neck and trousers was imminent.

The most difficult part he had to perform, however, was that of dissuading the bees, with the ends of his two fingers, from getting up his nostrils. These bees were not in good humour, as they were breathed upon, and were also deterred from doing as they pleased, and one bee showed his displeasure by stinging Mr Simmonds at the fork of his two fore fingers. This was not pleasant of itself; but it was a serious occurrence, as it might be the prelude to a more extensive attack. He avoided making any start when he was stung, and continued to push away as gently as possible those that were near his nostrils. On their return the hive was placed on three bricks with its mouth downwards, and Mr Simmonds slowly laid himself on the grass with his head close to the hive. The honey soon attracted the bees nearest to it, and a slow movement of the bees took place, till at length the whole swarm gradually gathered itself under and within the hive, except a few patches of bees which in walking away Mr Simmonds easily disengaged from his dress with his hand, and made them join their companions. Mr Simmonds thus escaped from not only a very disagreeable, but a perilous situation. It occupied three hours from the time that the bees alighted on their master to the time of his release.

Yrs., W. DRUMMOND,
Croydon, S.

1869

FISHING FOR CROCODILES

SIR, THERE IS A CHARMING illustration of crocodile catching in your last paper. It is not easy to say which is most to be admired, the pleasant nonchalance of the steersman, who is holding a walking-stick perpendicularly in the water at the stern of the boat, or the free action of the reptile advancing open-mouthed to its bow. Tourists investing in the tackle recommended will, whether they capture crocodiles or not, be certain of having a goose at each end of the line.

Yrs., 'AQUARIUS'

SIR, I AM PERHAPS ONE of the very few men who have fished successfully for alligators, and I have caught only seven. One of the largest (measuring 18 ft. 9 in., and in girth 11 ft. 3 in.) ran out 30 fathoms of 1½ in. white Manilla rope, and then dragged 27 men, the odd seven of whom were Europeans, up to their waists in mud and water, only giving in when choked by his mouth being kept open by the way in which he was hooked. The head of this alligator is now in my possession, and weighs 63 lb. Your correspondent's sketches and theories may catch the unwary sportsman, but I

Crocodile fishing on the Nile

question whether they will ever catch an alligator. I studied how to catch them in the Hooghly for years, and the only bait I ever found they would look at was the lights and lungs of a pig left with about 3 or 4 in. of windpipe attached, through which the bait was inflated, and so floated. The hook or hooks used were shark hooks, but not of the ordinary make. They must be fine steel, and very thick in the bend; ordinary shark hooks will straighten. I have one now, which did not catch, straightened, and even had the barb torn away. Add to this, there is, as far as I know, but one place where an alligator can be hooked securely, and that is at the back of the roof of the mouth. When the hook fixed there, and there only, were they landed. Two

hooks should be used, wired back to back, and the greatest possible care taken to conceal the hooks, for the beasts are as wily as foxes.

I write these few lines as a warning. No fishing in the world requires more patience. It will take six months to catch as many, and, when hooked, beware! They are the most powerful brutes in the water I ever tackled, and would walk away with and smash a fleet of boats, hoisting tackle and all, before you could say 'Jack Robinson'. Nothing under white Manilla, and that 1½ in., will hold them, and an ordinary shark hook will not. Shooting is of no use in the water.

Yrs., 'AN OLD INDIAN'

CITY GRAVEYARDS GONE TO POT

WHAT TO DO WITH OUR city graveyards is a very important question, particularly when considered in relation to the great wants of London and other large cities for open space, play, recreation and breathing grounds. Taking some interest in this question, we visited the large churchyard of Stepney on the 25th ult. The cemetery is a large one, and admirably capable of being converted into a charming pleasure ground or garden at a comparatively trifling expense; but the chief fact of practical interest that we have to record is that in one corner evidences of a highly practical nature betrayed themselves in the character of two small crops, clean and apparently pretty well looked after. One was mint, and the other hemp – this last not a

common object of cultivation in graveyards. A not inexcusable weakness for lamb on someone's part may account for the large provision of spearmint; but why a crop of *Cannabis sativa* over the graves in God's Acre at Stepney? We believe that an opium-smoking establishment is one of the many graces of the close, narrow courts in Bluegate Fields, and possibly among the Asiatics who visit the port of London there are enough passionately devoted to the 'leaf of pleasure' to cause a demand for the home grown article. But then we doubt the power of the Stepney summer to develop the potent and intoxicating churrus on the hemp, and are driven to the conclusion that it is the fibrous portions rather than the secretions of the hemp that Stepney

THE ELEVATOR GUN.

BRIEF DIRECTIONS FOR PURCHASERS.

The use of this Gun is so easily acquired that a child may shoot with it, if strict attention be given to the following directions:

Stand with the head erect, exactly as in archery. Screw the Elevator well up and grasp it firmly round the lower part with the left hand; then hold the gun with both arms extended, as in the figure. In taking sight, be sure to look along the *whole length of the gun.*

In firing for the first time, not more than half the usual sporting charge should be put into the gun, say one drachm of powder and half an ounce of shot.

At each successive shot the charge may be increased, so long as it is found that the recoil is under control.

An ounce of shot and two and a half drachms of powder may, after a little practice, be fired with perfect safety.

* If the shooter looks down upon the barrel instead of looking along it, the shot will pass over the mark aimed at.

CHARLES POMEROY BUTTON,
Nos. 142 & 143, CHEAPSIDE, LONDON.

THE HYDROPULT

IS

INVALUABLE FOR USE IN THE GARDEN

FOR

WATERING BEDS.

SPRINKLING PLANTS,

DROWNING OUT INSECTS,

CLEANSING TREES FROM SMUTS,

DRESSING WITH LIQUID MANURE,

&c. &c.

THE HYDROPULT

IS

DESIRABLE IN EVERY HOUSEHOLD

FOR

WASHING WINDOWS,

WETTING SIDEWALKS,

SPRINKLING STREETS,

WASHING CARRIAGES,

EMPTYING CISTERNS,

FILLING BARRELS,

A SPRAY BATH,

&c. &c.

PRICE £2. 2s.

Complete with 2½ feet Suction, and 3 feet Delivery Hose, Galvanised Wire Strainer, Bow, and Small Jet.

ORDERED BY THE WAR DEPARTMENT

AS FIRE ENGINES.

ROBERT HOGG, LL.D., and F.L.S., REV. H. H. DOMBRAIN, A. B. SHIRLEY HIBBERD, Esq., F.R.H.S., THOMAS RIVERS, Esq. (the eminent Florist), and other well-known gentlemen, recommend

THE HYDROPULT

AS AN

INVALUABLE GARDEN IMPLEMENT.

THE HYDROPULT WILL DRAW WATER HORIZONTALLY, IF NECESSARY, THROUGH TWO HUNDRED FEET SUCTION HOSE, AND FORCE IT THROUGH DELIVERY HOSE TO AN ALTITUDE OF ONE HUNDRED FEET.

THE HYDROPULT

EMPTYING CISTERNS — EXTINGUISHING A FIRE — PROTECTING ROOF

WASHING CARRIAGES

CLEANING WINDOWS — YACHTING PURPOSES

AN INVENTION FOR THROWING WATER BY HAND POWER

FILLING & EMPTYING BARRELS — CLEANSING TREES & SPRINKLING PLANTS — SPRINKLING SIDE WALKS

SHOW ROOMS,

Nos. 142 and 143,

CHEAPSIDE, LONDON.

EXTRACTS FROM THE PRESS.

THE HYDROPULT.—" The machine is certainly the most compact and efficacious force pump of its size that we have ever seen."—DAILY TELEGRAPH.

THE HYDROPULT.—" All Londoners and other town residents who care for their gardens and greenhouses, should avail themselves of such engines."—GARDENERS' CHRONICLE AND AGRICULTURAL GAZETTE.

THE HYDROPULT.—" We strongly recommend it to our readers."—JOURNAL OF HORTICULTURE AND COTTAGE GARDENER.

THE HYDROPULT.—" It will soon pay for its cost in a garden, besides being always at hand in case of an emergency of any kind which may require an immediate removal or discharge of water."—GARDENERS' WEEKLY MAGAZINE.

THE HYDROPULT.—" Country readers who order it on our recommendation, will not only not repent, but thank us for calling attention to a machine which, having once used, they will never care to be without."—FLORAL WORLD AND GARDEN GUIDE.

THE HYDROPULT.—" We can only say that no public establishment or private house should be without one of these useful machines."—COMMERCIAL DAILY LIST.

THE HYDROPULT.—" We are satisfied that all housekeepers ought to have one, and we are equally satisfied that if they once see it they will order it."—LIVERPOOL DAILY POST.

THE HYDROPULT.—" We commend it to the notice of the proprietors of warehouses and other buildings, public and private, in the metropolis and provinces."—MECHANICS' MAGAZINE.

THE HYDROPULT.—" We strongly recommend its use to all owners of manufactories, and to those householders who are not within easy hail of the ordinary fire-engines. It is admirably adapted for garden purposes. We have practically tested its efficacy in this way, and a more easy and effectual mode of irrigation cannot be conceived."—BIRMINGHAM JOURNAL.

THE HYDROPULT.—" We consider this appliance to be the most simple and effective form of portable fire-engine extant."—PORTSMOUTH TIMES AND NAVAL GAZETTE.

THE HYDROPULT.—" It will be an inexcusable negligence in housekeepers who fail to keep a Hydropult in the corner of the kitchen, or in some other convenient part of their premises."—FORT MAGAZINE.

THE HYDROPULT.—" * * * As to the principle of this pump, we consulted the highest living authority, who reported very favourably."—INSURANCE GAZETTE.

The above testimonials are selected from some hundreds which this invaluable instrument has received.

CAUTION!
IMPORTANT TO THE PUBLIC.

The extensive sale of the HYDROPULT has excited the cupidity of so-called respectable, but in reality unprincipled manufacturers, who are now palming on the public worthless imitations of the HYDROPULT, and through their connections are enabled to place said devices on exhibition, and for sale, in many of the principal Ironmongery and Seed Establishments throughout the city and provinces. These devices resemble in many respects the HYDROPULT in appearance, and are calculated to deceive the unsuspecting. The Proprietor therefore issues this Caution, and respectfully intimates that parties wishing to purchase the HYDROPULT should examine the machine offered for sale, and see if it has attached thereto a label, with the following words: "THE HYDROPULT, VOSE'S Patent, manufactured only by GRIFFITHS and BROWETT, Birmingham. CHARLES POMEROY BUTTON, Proprietor, 142 and 143, Cheapside, London." Unless this label is attached, the Machine is not the HYDROPULT.

owes its graveyard crop. Possibly it may be a caution to the parishioners! In one part we observed a much decayed tombstone, bearing a date more than two hundred years old, holding up its head amidst the crop, as if making a vain protest against the latest shabby novelty that we are acquainted with in graveyard gardening.

HARE

SIR, ONE DAY, A SHORT time ago, a farm servant of William Taylor's, at Harum, Yorkshire, was ploughing when he caught a young hare and proceeded to earmark it. He had marked one ear, the young hare screamed loudly, and the old hare (which he had not previously noticed) flew up at him and severely tore his hands, then she remained within a few feet of him till he turned the young one down again. This is boldness on the part of a usually very timid animal not often met with.

Yrs., 'DRUID'

SUPPOSED OCCURRENCE OF THE PASSENGER PIGEON IN DERBYSHIRE

SIR, I HAVE GREAT REASON to suppose that an individual of this species, so rarely met with in England, was shot near Melbourne a short time ago. The keeper of N. Curzon, Esq, who has the shooting over that parish, observing an unusual bird flying out of the 'Intake' at the back of Melbourne Pool, fired at and killed it. It was very much mutilated, and was put away as unfit for preservation. He described the bird so exactly to me that I felt sure in my own mind what bird it was. However, I said nothing about it, but showed him fine coloured drawings of all our known wild pigeons. He could not identify it until we came to that of the passenger pigeon, when he at once identified it as the bird which he had shot. As I did not see the species myself, I cannot give a decided opinion of the species, but I have no doubt in my own mind that it was that of the passenger pigeon.

Yrs., JOHN JOSEPH BRIGGS,
King's Newton, Swarkeston,
Derby

LARKS

SIR, I NOTICED TODAY A circumstance with reference to this bird that I should have deemed impossible to have taken place, viz. the bird can sing – and sing well – even whilst it is holding food for its young in its mouth. One hovered over my head for a considerable time, having apparently a small worm in its bill, and yet trilling out its notes with as much ease as if its mandibles were not encumbered.

Yrs., JOHN JOSEPH BRIGGS

HOBBY/TERN

SIR, I OBSERVED A VERY fine female hobby flying about this place on Monday the 23rd May. She came all but within shot, but, as my piece was charged with No. 10, for the summer warblers etc., I did not fire. On the 25th, I saw either a black or a sooty tern – I am not sure which – near Horley, on the Brighton line.

Yrs., F.S.D.,
'The Firs', nr. Hampstead

BLACKBIRD

SIR, IS IT GENERALLY KNOWN that the *Meruli-dae* void the stones and pips by the mouth or bill? This is new to me, although I have studied the habits of birds for many years.

Yrs., CRICHTON

[This is not invariably the case, as we have positive evidence to the contrary: we do not distrust our correspondent, but hope he will repeat the observation, and let us know the result. In the blackbird, thrush, and missel-thrush the pips or stones *commonly* pass with the excrement. – Ed.]

GOLD-COLOURED EEL

SIR, THERE IS, AT THIS present time, to be seen alive, at the Horse and Groom, Beccles, a very singular specimen of an eel. It is about 13 or 14 inches in length, and of a bright golden colour, similar to a gold-fish. I have seen many a bright coloured eel, but never anything approaching to the one I have mentioned. I am told it was caught with an eel-pritch in Oulton Broad, near Lowestoft. Have any of your readers seen a similar one?

Yrs., J.F.

[This is a very unusual variety. Eels are remarkable for their uniformity of colour, and we cannot speak, like our correspondent, of having seen many a brightly coloured one. – Ed.]

Sir, As Mr James was fishing in the river Wharfe, about a mile below Otley, on Tuesday last, he caught an eel 14 inches long and 6 ounces in weight, of a bright golden colour, the belly white. It can be seen at Mr Earnshaw's, Borogate, Otley, who has had it preserved.

Yrs., P.,
Otley, Yorkshire

SINGING MOUSE

SIR, WHEN HOUSE SURGEON at St George's Hospital, I had a veritable singing mouse. The day of the Duke of Wellington's funeral the sofa was occupied by a friend from Bristol. In the morning he came in with a long face and a long story about some odd noise in the cupboard which kept him awake half the night. It was the singing mouse, who had been piping away right merrily. This mouse was caught in the College-hall at Westminster, and given me by the College butler. In one of his lectures Professor Owen stated that the mouse, in its anatomy, approaches closely to the bird, and that we should not be surprised that the voice is 'bird-like' in some instances.

The note of my mouse was a very pretty bird-like twitter; he only sang at night and ceased at the least noise; and I maintain that my mouse was not a 'wheezy' mouse, nor yet 'thick in the wind'.

Yrs., F.T. BUCKLAND

SINGING SNAILS

SIR, NOISES AT NIGHT, often attributed to 'singing mice', may be caused by the friction of the shells of snails in their passage over the glass of a window. Singularly, whilst reading of the 'singing mouse' on Saturday evening last, I heard similar sounds as those described proceeding from the window, and on pulling up the blind I saw a couple of snails drawing themselves along and, at intervals, scraping the glass with their shells. Of course the scraping of the shells on a large pane of glass would produce a different tone from that on a small one. I knew an old lady who was terrified for several nights by sounds which were eventually found to proceed from itinerant snails.

Yrs., G.R.M.,
Durrance Farm, Rickmansworth

1870

HIRED SERVANTS

A SUBJECT REQUIRING MORE attention than it usually receives is the supervision bestowed on hired servants. Too often they are allowed to spend their evenings abroad, without the master taking the trouble to enquire as to their whereabouts; hence it often happens that young men acquire a taste for gambling and bad society. In old times all the members of a farm household lived together, and the lads were continually under their master's supervision. Some attempt should be made to provide amusement for the lads of a winter's evening. The men's apartments should be above the kitchen approached by a ladder staircase, and detached from the rest of the house. We cannot say too much as to the importance of this. The immorality prevalent in Cumberland and Westmorland, where the labourers are comparatively well educated and well paid, may be greatly attributed to defective accommodation in farm houses. We venture on one quotation from the commissioner's report: 'The sleeping accommodation from the farm houses has long been a disgrace to these counties; and, although some improvement has taken place in this respect within the last 20 years, the same stairs often lead to the rooms of both male and female servants. Only a few years ago, in one of the largest farm houses in the district, belonging to one of the principal landed proprietors, the men and women servants slept in the same room – the men at one end, the women at the other with not even a curtain to separate them; and in another case, a farmer apologising for the domestic

Old Holmes, of Eye, a Suffolk farm worker of mid-Victorian times

arrangements of his house, said he had done the best he could for the protection of his female servants by putting curtains to their beds.' With every care and precau-tion, the farmer will find it difficult at times to keep his servants right; but with such shocking accommodation as the above, we can only look for gross immorality.

THE TAY

SIR, THERE HAVE BEEN TWO remarkable captures on the Tay during the past few days. One was that of a seal, measuring fully 6 ft. long and weighing 40 stone, which took place on Thursday the 10th March at a station in the estuary belonging to Mr Speedie, of Perth, one of the leading tacksmen on the river. It was brought up alive to Perth next day, and exhibited to wondering crowds till it was shot on the following Saturday evening. The same trap which was invented by Mr Speedie has been the destruction of many large seals during the last five years. The other event was the capture, by Mr John Haggard, of a magnificent salmon of 61 lb., at Stanley after a long and hard struggle. This salmon was the heaviest which had been caught, either by rod or net, in the Tay during the present century; and it is also a remarkable fact that so large a fish should have been taken at this early period of the season.

Yrs., 'TAVUS'

1871

THE CORNISH CHOUGH

SIR, THIS HANDSOME BIRD, though less numerous in this locality than it was 40 years ago, is yet far from being extinct; indeed, they seem of late to be on the increase. Being very destructive (or believed to be so by farmers) to the young wheat plant, continual war is waged with them in the autumn and winter months, which consequently thins them off. Specimens, also, are called for now for taxidermists very much oftener than formerly. Several pairs annually build their nests in the ruins of our episcopal palace, and that of St Mary's College – the ruined tower of the latter being a favourite place with them – but for the last five years the bustle and the noise consequent on the repairs of the cathedral have scared them away, and they now nest in the sea-shore cliffs. I often see ten or a dozen together, sometimes more, but more often in pairs.

Yrs., SAMUEL WILLIAMS,
St David's

GREAT BUSTARD ON SALISBURY PLAIN

SIR, AFTER A LAPSE OF SOME 50 years, a bustard has been shot on Salisbury plain. It was shot yesterday on Mr Lywood's farm, near Yarnborough Castle, an old Roman encampment, about 3 miles N.E. of Wylye station on the Salisbury branch of the Great Western Railway. It was being exhibited in Salisbury today, but I did not hear of it until I was on the point of leaving the town. My informant tells me he thought it was a young hen bird, as far as he could judge, and that there were two others in company with it when shot. It is in the possession of Mr Stevens, of Salisbury, who I have no doubt will have it preserved and add it to his interesting museum.

Yrs., JOHN WYNDHAM,
Sutton Mandeville, Salisbury

FARM LABOURERS AND THE FROST

SIR, ALLOW ME TO CALL the attention of your readers to a sad grievance the farm labourer suffers from, and one worthy, I think, of the notice of Parliament. As soon as the frost sets in, it is the custom among many farmers to turn off a portion of their men, who then have to go to the work-house for relief. Many of these men have slaved on the same farm for years, and are to be taken on again as soon as the frost breaks up. Supposing a long frost, as is now the case, the poor fellows are for a time half starved, and perhaps the germs of disease sown, and they become at some future time a burden to their parish.

What would farmers say were gentlemen to send off their under-gardeners to be kept by the ratepayers during frost?

The remedy I propose is this, that the regular labourer on any farm, on being dismissed, should receive from his employer a month's notice or a month's wage.

The farmer then, not being able to guess how long a frost would last, would employ the men in hedging and road making on the farm; thereby the farm would be improved, and the labourers would escape being pauperised.

Yrs., 'YORICK'

Sir, As a farmer, I must protest against this charge by 'Yorick'. He can have little acquaintance with the subject about which he writes, or he would know that there is very much work on a farm which is generally reserved for a frost – the carting of manure, etc. – and also that during such times much more labour is required in getting together the food for sheep and cattle. In this way all the men are kept well employed.

No; the men who flock to the work-houses during a frost are not the regular labourers of a farm, but men of an inferior class, some of whom are too ignorant, and others too idle and worthless, ever to secure permanent employment.

Yrs., 'NORTH LINCOLN'

WEASEL ON LOCH SHIN

SIR, A PARTY OF FRIENDS and myself were lately staying at Overscaig Inn, about 2 miles from the head of Loch Shin in Sutherlandshire, when, between seven and eight o'clock in the evening, we observed a wave, caused evidently by the swimming of an animal, so small that even with the aid of a field glass we could not discern it. The animal was crossing in a straight line from the opposite side of the loch. An old boatman, Sandy Ross, was despatched to meet it on its reaching the bank, and he brought back a young weasel as a trophy. The loch was fully half a mile broad, and the little creature took about 20 minutes to accomplish its enterprising but perilous journey. None of the small population at Overscaig remembered such an incident having occurred before; but a traditional anecdote was told by Ross, the boatman above referred to, and who has spent a long life in the district, to the effect that a weasel had once been seen to take to the water when pursued by a snake, which, however, it did not escape, as the reptile followed in its wake, and, after they had both crossed the loch, succeeded in capturing its prey.

Yrs., J.W.D.,
Edinburgh

THE CLIFTON-NONPAREIL MOTH

Sir, Some of your entomological readers may be interested to hear that yesterday afternoon (Sunday, 10 September) I saw a remarkably fine and perfect specimen of the rare 'Clifton Non-pareil' moth (*Catocala fraxini*). When I first perceived it, it was at rest on the warm western front of this house, over one of the lower windows. I pointed it out to some of the members of Mr Burr's family, thinking it was the common C. *napta* or red underwing, when to my great astonishment it spread its wings, exposing the blue under-one, fluttering over the string course for a few moments, and then took flight. After flying round me several times, it pitched again at a higher elevation, remained a while with its wings expanded, and then, gradually closing them, settled down for the remainder of its afternoon nap. I give you all this detail that entomologists may know what amount of trust to place in this observation of an insect not actually captured. It was no passing glance, being in my sight five minutes at least. I was a very keen collector of English lepidoptera some six or seven and twenty years ago, and would have gone half mad over such a chance to capture what was then considered a most rare British insect. I do not know if it is thought so much of now. I should think the exquisite park in which this house is situated eminently adapted for entomology. Broken into hill and dale, breezy heath and ferny dell, studded with noble oaks of vast size and age in all their strength and vigorous health, and in all the beauty of picturesque decay, chestnuts, beeches, birches, elms, every British and numberless foreign trees; ponds almost large enough to be called lakes, nourishing on their margins the rushes, reeds, and grasses of various climes; while the waters of the river Kennet

Soft and slow
Amid the verdant landscape flow –
such is Aldermaston!

Yrs., E.L. LAYARD

1872

A GOOD STORY AUTHENTICATED

SIR, THE PARAGRAPH WHICH appeared in your last edition about the late Mr John Claudius Loudon does not give a correct version of the amusing incident alluded to in it. The facts were these:

Whilst Mr Loudon was preparing his great work called the 'Arboretum' he wrote to the Duke of Wellington the following letter:

J.C. Loudon presents his compliments to the Duke of Wellington, and will feel obliged if his Grace will give permission for the inspection of his celebrated Waterloo beeches.

The Duke, on receiving this letter, imagined it to be from the Bishop of London, whose signature 'C.J. London,' much resembled that of J.C. Loudon, the handwriting also being similar. The Duke, with his usual promptitude, immediately wrote to the Bishop of London the following letter:

F.M. the Duke of Wellington presents his compliments to the Bishop of London, and begs to say that, although the articles mentioned by the Bishop of London are no longer in existence, the Bishop is at liberty to inspect any other article of apparel belonging to the Duke.

The Duke appears to have read Mr Loudon's word 'beeches' as 'breeches' and, thinking that the Bishop of London must have been *non compos* when he wrote the letter, after replying to the Bishop, mounted his horse and went to the house of Sir Robert Peel, then Prime Minister.

To his Grace's astonishment, on arriving at Sir Robert Peel's residence, he found the Bishop of London there with his (the Duke's) letter, he having gone to the Prime Minister for the purpose of consulting as to the state of the Duke's mind, which he (the Bishop) naturally supposed to be out of order.

The explanation which is said to have taken place before Sir Robert Peel was as amusing as satisfactory.

The incident was mentioned in the papers at the time with various versions; but the above is a correct account as given by the late Mrs Loudon, and therefore may be relied on.

Yrs., M.S.

1873

THE NEGRO

SIR, I DON'T KNOW WHETHER an English labourer would work or not if he was not forced to do so; probably he would not. But, for all that, I do know that a negro will not work, even when he can by so doing earn more than his actual wants require. There's the point. I am inclined to think that an average English labourer would.

I have lived nine years constantly among 'niggers' and 'greasers'. A gaucho is far more brutal than a negro; but the latter is by far the cruellest person I know. Let me explain. A gaucho lacks the feeling of humanity, as Darwin observes. He will thrust a knife between the horns, or put out the eye of an ox, and think nothing of it – he knows no better. A negro knows very well what he is about. I heard myself, only three months ago, at Jamaica, on the way to the Moneague, some fearful yells emanating from a cottage perched on the side of the hillside. I pulled up, and, on pushing aside the branches, there was an old woman holding down a boy in a large wooden tub, while over him stood a stout nigger with a stick. The boy was completely covered with 'yaws' – small ulcers the size of a shilling. A third woman was literally scraping these with some leafy shrub, and every time the poor wretch howled the man beat him savagely. I am not very big, and not particularly strong, but I felt inclined to see if I had forgotten Alec Keene's lessons. I quite agree with 'Ethiopia's' opinion of agricultural labourers in England. After ten years' incessant travelling, I know no class of people anywhere so degraded. But, thank God, there seems a brighter prospect.

Yrs., OLIVER NORTH

GLENGARRY BOOTS

SIR, CAN ANY OF YOUR readers who have worn the porpoise hide Glengarry boots give any other than a favourable judgement of their waterproof properties? From the favourable opinions of the boots of some of your correspondents which you have at times published I was induced to order a pair, but my experience, I regret to say, differs widely from that of some of your more fortunate sporting friends; for

amongst wet grass or turnips after an hour's beat I am not a whit better off than if I went forth in my carpet slippers, and, as a consequence colds and sore throats have been through this season the order of the day: this, after paying two guineas for boots, is very disheartening. I am about to re-order, and my object in writing to you, Sir, is to ascertain if I am the only unlucky speculator in porpoise, as, of course, I am quite aware that the best of workmen in all trades are sometimes deceived in the quality of materials they get hold of. I must, however, add that I have written on the subject to the manager of the company who make these boots – not indeed asking for compensation but only requiring a guarantee against any future mishap of the kind; but that 'gentleman' does not deign to make me any reply, although I forwarded him a stamped directed envelope for the purpose. This, however, is no surprise to me; it agrees with my former experience of a few other London tradesmen I could mention. Any of your correspondents who will kindly give me some information on the subject will confer a favour on

Yrs., 'AGOL'

Sir, I have had a pair of porpoise hide boots from the Co-operative Boot Company which fitted me easily from the first, so much so that I had no need to employ a man to wear them ten days or so before me. I have worn them in all weathers, and highly approve of them. They are quite waterproof; I have worn them in all weathers for two winters, and knocked about in them in the Tyrol for several weeks.

Yrs., W. HARPER,
Bury, Lancashire

Sir, I bought a pair of Glengarry boots in September 1871. I have worn them for sporting purposes ever since, both for shooting and fishing, and I can say most truthfully they are the best boots ever made; their waterproof qualities are undeniable, and if there is any fault to find with them, they are too comfortable. I know nothing of the company. I sent my measurement to them, and they sent the boots, for which they were paid. Perhaps 'Agol' failed to use the oil for their preservation.

Yrs., JOSEPH SAW,
Alpha Villa, South Brent, Devon

1874

NASSAU, BAHAMAS

SIR, HAVING BEEN A RESIDENT for some years in the Bahamas, I am in a position to give your correspondent G.C.G. the information he requires. With regard to his first question, I should say that Nassau was decidedly not suitable for hotel keeping, there being already a large hotel on the island, the accommodation of which is in excess of that required. As for an orange plantation, I am not so well qualified to judge, not having paid much attention to the subject; but I do not believe it would succeed in a profitable point of view. The climate of the Bahamas is warm, but generally healthy; the town of Nassau clean, healthy, and picturesque; yellow fever, however, being an occasional visitant.

Yrs., C.T. FITZGERALD

LAWN TENNIS

SIR, I HAVE LATELY SEEN a new game played which will be a great acquisition as an out-door amusement at country houses. The game is called Sphairistike, or Lawn Tennis; the rules are very simple and clear.

Yrs., GERALD D. FITZGERALD,
42 Grosvenor-place, London

DEATH WATCHES

SIR, THESE ARE SOMETIMES found where the application of boiling water would be particularly inconvenient. I have met with the insect in a piano, whether in the works or in the case I could not quite make out. In another instance it had chosen for its quarters the frame of an engraving hanging against the panelled wall of a room in the Neville Court of Trinity, Cambridge. The occupant of the room was a good deal

annoyed by the ticking, which sounded all the louder on account of the resonance of the sound board behind the frame, and it was resolved to make the beetle tick itself to death. The picture was accordingly taken down, and a watch laid upon it and kept going. The insect will always respond to the tick of a watch or the tap of a finger-nail; and for about two days, if I remember rightly, Mrs (or Mr? – do not both sexes tick and challenge each other?) *Anobium* incessantly replied to her supposed rival (or sweetheart); but at length she caved in, and was heard no more. The 'death tick' and the beat of the escapement could be clearly distinguished when both were going together.

Yrs., C.J.G.,
Bury St Edmunds

1882

THE CHANNEL TUNNEL

WE MUST CONFESS THAT we have never regarded with much favour the project of making a submarine tunnel between England and the Continent. We do not speak of the difficulties of the undertaking. Probably the opponents of the scheme have as much overestimated, as its promoters have underestimated them. Were they as gigantic as some have predicted, we can quite believe that, given the necessary funds, the combined skill of French and English engineers would be equal to the task of overcoming them. Nor are we influenced by any such feelings of sentimental patriotism as those which led the late Lord Palmerston to deprecate that great achievement of M. de Lesseps – the Suez Canal. Our main objection to the undertaking is that, assuming it to be made, there seems, on the one hand, a very small likelihood of sufficient traffic passing through it to render it a paying concern, while, on the other, the chance of such an easy communication between us and the neighbouring nation proving, under certain circumstances, a real danger to this country, appears to us one not to be despised, or to be lightly dismissed. Estimates of the amount of passenger and goods traffic which will be taken by preference under the sea rather than over it, can afford no clue to the solution of the financial question until some reasonable approximation to the actual cost of the tunnel is arrived at.

1883

BEADS FOR AFRICAN BARTER

SIR, CAN ANY OF YOUR readers inform me where the coloured beads, used by explorers in trading with the natives in the interior of Africa, can be obtained?

Yrs., 'CRYSTAL'

[Our correspondent will find a list of 35 bead sellers in Kelly's Post Office London Directory, of whom 13 are also importers (such as Lewin, 1, Bevis Marks). Two sorts of beads are used for barter with the natives, made of glass and porcelain; the first are manufactured at Venice, and could possibly be obtained through the London agents of the Venice Glass Company at 30, St James's-street. But it is absolutely necessary to warn 'Crystal' that if he wants beads for use in an exploring or shooting expedition, his success will depend on his having the very latest fashion, which constantly changes; and he must therefore get his stock at the nearest supplying station on the coast, where the first news of the kinds of bead in vogue is received from the interior, and where explorers fit themselves out from the stores of local traders. The expression 'interior of Africa' is, of course, subject to the route taken from the east, west, or south coast, on each of which the fashion would differ according to the tribes met with.

One of the most recent successful travellers, Mr Joseph Thomson, at pages 35 and 36 of volume one of his work, *To the Central African Lakes and Back*, describes the mutability of the African taste in the way of beads; depending on the knowledge supposed to be possessed by Chuma, the well-tried attendant of Livingstone, who accompanied him, he laid in a considerable supply of beads of the required size, composition and colour, only to find them utterly useless, after a laborious and costly transportation. The extra cost of buying off a middleman must be accepted without hesitation; it will be better than paying the expenses of transit from home with the almost inevitable result of finding the stock unmarketable rubbish, hardly accepted as a present, as Mr Thomson did. Of course, if the object is purely trade, it would be impossible to turn a profit unless the goods were bought at first price; but such commercial details would scarcely be within the province of *The Field*, and we could scarcely open our columns for a discussion of them. Such firms as Messrs Gray, Dawes, and Co., 13 Austin Friars, as regards the east coast trade at all events, would in all probability know them, but would also in all probability decline to impart information to be used commercially against the traders whom they represent. – Ed.]

BARBED WIRE FENCING

SIR, MANY PEOPLE, MORE especially hunting men, have been for some time anxiously waiting to hear opinions expressed upon the new barbed wire fencing now coming into use. What will its effect on hunting be? If it comes into general use I think there can be no two opinions on the subject that hunting will be doomed. 'Stockman' in your issue of last week, gives us a synopsis of its effects, and they have a

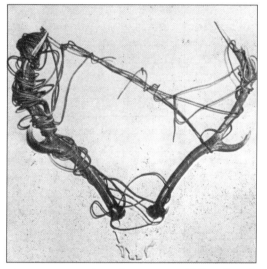

A warning to tidy up loose wire – 40 lb. of steel wire festooned round a stag's antlers

very ugly ring about them. 'It will tear a horse to pieces,' he says, and 'Cut pieces of hide a foot square' out of them. I think few men would care to risk themselves or their horses in a country where such pleasant surprises as these are liable to take place. Imagine also hounds racing with a breast-high scent, and coming crash at such an obstacle. Ugh! the very thought of it is sickening. The common wire has terrors enough; but its effects will be dwarfed into insignificance by the monster now threatening us. Looking at it from a farmer's point of view, it appears to me that its use would occasion more losses by accidents to his cattle and horses than he would benefit by the lesser cost and longer durability of the fence. Apart from cattle and horses, it would be a serious loss to him by tearing the wool from sheep. On short-woolled sheep its effect would probably not be so bad; but I cannot answer for its consequences upon long wools, such as Leicesters, Cheviots, and Blackfaces. Of course nothing can be done to stop its use; but much may be done to check it by the condemnation of public opinion, which I doubt not will be forthcoming.

Yrs., G.G, Doddington

THE LEA

SIR, IS THE FOLLOWING worth recording? Early in April 1825 I caught a brace of salmon in the river Lea, one 6¾ lb., the other 4½ lb. weight. At that time it was

considered a slice of luck to take two in a day, and as a boy I was rather proud of the job. I cannot call to mind the exact locality, but I recollect I put my pony up at a dyehouse at Old Ford, walked upstream, and paid one shilling for the liberty of fishing. They were caught with a worm on a single gut. I went to sea soon after, and have not visited the locality since, so I do not know whether there are any there now.

Yrs., F. DAVEY

[You might possibly catch a dead dog or a kitten, but no salmon has been there for thirty years or more. – Ed.]

RAT HUNTING

Sir, When rat hunting I always carry a long cavalry sword, which pierces the banks more effectually than any spear.

Yrs., C.E.R.

TUG OF WAR – BOAT *v* LAND

Sir, Those of your readers who take an interest in athletics would, no doubt, be glad to hear of a tug of war between four men in a boat and four men on land, which we had at Malta a short time ago. The tug of war originated by a discussion after dinner, when most of us were in favour of the men in the boat winning. We therefore determined to try it out practically. Eight good strong men were picked out, and four of them put into the boat, the rope having been made fast to the stern. The other end of the rope was held on shore by the other four men, and on a signal both pulled together. About 20 yds. separated the two teams, and although the men in the boat rowed their hardest, still the men on land simply ran away with them without the least exertion. We then tried two men on land, and this time gave the boat a running start. On the word being given, the two men picked up the rope, which was dragging along the ground, and hauled in the boat with the greatest ease, although the four in the boat were pulling with all their might.

Selecting a big strong man, we tried him, and, as he won so easily, we picked out a drummer-boy of about 15, and not a particularly strong boy either. This time the boat was given a longer running start, and the rope, very muddy and slippery, was dragging along the ground pretty sharply, when the boy was told to lay on. The boat stopped at once as if it had hit a rock, and slowly the boy pulled it to the shore despite the utmost endeavours of its rowers. The ground was very wet and slippery, the rope the same, and the boy in his bare feet, and yet the four rowers were powerless to prevent themselves being pulled ashore. Every plan was tried, by keeping the oars in the water etc., but not one of them was of any use.

The boat was a large and heavy four-oared company boat; the rope was not a very heavy one, being only about an inch and a quarter diameter; and there was no wind to speak of.

The result astonished some of us not a little, as no one had ever seen it tried before.

Yrs., 'SUBALTERN',
Malta

FIELD MOUSE EJECTED BY BEE

SIR, A FEW DAYS AGO ONE of my sons captured a good-sized bumble bee on the flower of a large convolvulus, and, knowing of a mouse's hole just outside my garden lawn, we at once proceeded to the spot, to try the experiment of bolting the mouse. After introducing the bee into its temporary prison (the mouth of the hole), I placed my handkerchief quickly over until I heard a vigorous buzzing, when I removed the handkerchief and stepped back a few paces. Within a few moments, out darted a mouse, and disappeared into a second hole with such speed, that it was impossible to ascertain whether it was of the long or short-tailed species. The bumble bee emerged immediately afterwards, and reminded me most forcibly of the sport of ferretting rabbits. I have not since repeated the experiment, but I am told it is usually successful with a good, lively bee.

Yrs., JAMES CARTER

DAIRY PRODUCE AND THE PARCELS POST

SIR, I AM A SMALL DAIRY farmer, and sell at the rate of from 40 lb. to 50 lb. of butter every week, packed in half hundredweight tubs, for the English market. It seems to me that the new postal arrangements would enable me to supply several families, whose consumption would not exceed the postal limit, with good fresh butter at a lower price than they now pay for very bad; but I am at a loss to know how to avail myself of any of the packing cases which I see noticed in your paper. Not having seen them I do not understand how I could be supplied at moderate prices, unless they were so contrived as to fit into one another as hampers, which a game dealer in Manchester sends me for carrying rabbits, so that a customer could once in three months or so send off a package of empties. Perhaps some of your correspondents might be able to solve my difficulty.

At present we are getting in the market for salted butter 121s. 4d. per cwt., that is 13d. per lb. From this has to be deducted the price of the tub and market expenses, which in all comes to nearly 1d. per lb., if we do not happen to have more than a single tub to sell. So that 1s. 4d. per lb. would pay well enough if packages could be got at moderate rates, and my own know-ledge of London enables me to say that eatable butter is very seldom to be got at a much higher figure at any period of the year. In winter our prices rise with the English market to 16d. or 17d., rarely to 18d.; but at that season eatable butter is indeed a rarity in London, even at 2s. a lb. which I paid last April.

It is not unlikely that other farmers may think this subject worthy of consideration. I shall, at any rate, when I have made arrangements, give the course I propose a trial.

Yrs., 'DAIRY'

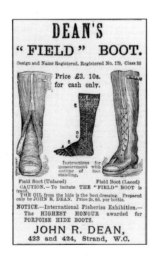

1886

PREFERENCE OF DONKEY FOR THISTLES

SIR, MOST PEOPLE ARE FAMILIAR with the saying that 'a donkey prefers thistle to corn because he's an ass,' but few probably, like myself, have any idea that the statement has any basis in fact. I have a young donkey (rising 2) out at grass, and during the recent hard weather having given instructions that he should have some chaff and corn; on being told that he, as far as possible, picked out the chaff and left the corn, I yesterday had some chaff, bran and crushed oats placed in three baskets and given to him, when he verified his proverbial peculiarity by eating the former and leaving both the latter. I had some idea of getting him into good condition next season with a view to see what he would do in carrying a little boy to hounds, but from this it would appear to be difficult to get him into the necessary condition. It would be interesting to know if any of your readers have had a similar experience.

Yrs., D.R.

RESUSCITATION OF GOLD FISH

SIR, I APPEND A COPY OF part of a letter which I received from my brother in Aberdeen (Mr R.D. Milne) this morning: 'We have all been very much excited over one of our gold fishes which are kept in a bowl in the dining-room. After breakfast yesterday morning the housemaid, when dusting behind the sideboard, came across something, which on inspection turned out to be our black gold fish, as dry and hard as a bone. It had been there so long that its skin had all blistered and peeled off; and, in its struggles, it had also chipped off half its tail and most of its fins. We put it in water and brandy and it revived! and by evening it could swim about a little. This morning, however, it was dead, its tail never having become a bit less hard than at first. The butler thinks, from traces of scale on a certain cloth, that it had been behind the sideboard all night, having jumped overboard shortly after our dinner; and it certainly looked it. So you see your story of sending gold fish from London, and reviving them, may be quite true; for if this one had not knocked itself about so much, I believe it would have recovered.'

Yrs., J.A. MILNE

FEROCITY IN A RABBIT

SIR, ON THE EVENING OF 27 April my son and I were watching the rabbits playing round a burrow in a field adjoining the house, and were astonished to see an old rabbit rush at a small one of probably 4 or 5 weeks old, seize it by the head, and, leaping from the ground, with one kick of its hind legs completely disembowelled it. The smaller rabbit had only sufficient life left to give a few convulsive struggles, while the old one at once resumed its previous employment of nibbling the grass. On picking up the small rabbit, we found its stomach was ripped up from one end to the other.

Yrs., L.M.

1888

OSTRICH IN MERSEY

SIR, AT NOON ON 4 JULY , as H.M. Customs' steam launch was returning to her mooring at the north-end of the landing stage, a strange object was discovered in the water. On nearing, it was found to be an enormous bird, which was at once transferred to the congenial warmth of the fore cabin. Though in an exhausted condition, it soon revived, and seemed to enjoy the food supplied. It was conjectured that it had strayed from the Eastham Zoological Gardens. Mr Thomson, the proprietor, was at once communicated with. He pronounced it to be a young ostrich, but not one of his collection. Whence it came is unknown. The Mersey has lately been characterised by the presence of unwelcome sharks, but an ostrich in the river is certainly a *rara avis*.

Yrs., T.C.A.

LARGE SALMON

SIR, ON 27 OCTOBER, 1886, I had, I believe, the grandest day's fishing ever recorded in England, Scotland or Ireland. It was in the upper Floors water of the Tweed. Up to 4 o'clock I had killed 14 fish, from 10 lb. up to 32 lb., when at the top of a stream called the Shott, I hooked a fish that had all its own way for an hour. It went eventually downstream, and at last showed itself by rushing across, breaking the water for the first time. It then gave symptoms of answering to the bit, and in 10 minutes was cleverly landed by the fisherman. Before dinner it was weighed by candlelight, in the presence of the guests in the castle, and pronounced to be over 60 lb. It was then wiped and cleaned up, and placed on a large tray in the entrance hall, for the benefit of those expected for dinner. The next morning its weight was declared to be 57½ lb. This fish was killed with a fly known as the Wilkinson.

Yrs., ARTHUR PRYOR,
Hylands

1890

LIZARD IN BANANAS

SIR, AT DINNER, MY BROTHER, whilst cutting a banana from a bunch of the fruit, discovered a live foreign lizard between the layers. It appears perfectly healthy, and is a dark brown colour with black markings, a large flat head, and feet with five toes, with flat ends to them, like those of a fly. It is about 5 in. long.

Yrs., B.B.H.,
Lymington

A lion shot on a settler's farm in northern Rhodesia

1891

LADIES ON HORSEBACK

Sir, I am sure I am echoing the ideas of the vast majority of no-horsey-fast women when I say that it would be a fatal mistake ever to let the fashion of women riding astride like men spread. One has only to look at a field in, say, Lincolnshire, to see what splendid horsewomen there are, who ride straight and fearlessly, and whose horses' backs do not get sore more often than the mounts of their brothers and husbands. I am sure there are already far too many girls who are inclined to be as manly as their brothers without encouragement that would be afforded by their dressing like men in the hunting-field. Besides, the thing that is generally very near a woman's heart, her appearance, would not be improved by donning man's attire completely. Let us be women first, and sportswomen next. What can be more becoming than a perfect-fitting habit on a well-corseted figure? – sitting upright and squarely on the saddle, with good well-fitting gloves and boots complete – a *tout ensemble* that no covert coat and breeches can equal. A slim waisted figure would look ridiculous in conjunction with a man's saddle.

Yrs., 'KEEN BUT FEMININE RIDER'

DECEMBER HARVEST

Sir, The ice harvestmen have been very busy at work in the past month. All the ponds of the metropolitan area have been, when possible, requisitioned for the rough ice formed in the night, which has been broken up, and in vanloads, cartloads, truckloads and barrowloads taken to some of the ice-wells, where the owner is ready to buy all that is brought. At about 2s. per load, the ice harvestmen can get a living; and, at 2s. per cwt. in summer, the ice merchant middleman is reckoned to make a profit of £100 from his stores, that hold 2,000 or 3,000 tons.

Yrs., 'QUI VIVE'

YOUNG ENGLISHMEN IN AUSTRALIA

SIR, A SOCIAL QUESTION OF some import-ance is the utterly reckless way in which young men are drafted off from England to Australia. Not a steamer reaches us in the colonies without bringing scores of these unfortunates, who are simply run out of their homes by their parents. The situa-tions they occupy in the colonies are potato peelers at inferior hotels, washers up at sixpenny restaurants, billiard markers and similar degrading and inferior pos-itions. In all the cities, and in the bush towns they are the outcasts of our civilis-ations, without money and without a trade. In some cases they bring out with them, say, £100. They put up at the best hotel, bring letters of introduction (which count for very little in the colonies), wear patent leathers and an eyeglass, and go through their small hoard in magnificent style. From the hotel they descend to 'apartments', thence to the cheap boarding house, and so on down to the Domain (public park), where they may be found in every stage of squalor, dirt, and wretched-ness. Perhaps they manage to get into the country or into Northern Queensland, where the end comes quickly from rum and fever. Here in Sydney, in the Domain, are Vandaleurs, Talbots, De Courcys, Stan-leys, Fitzosbornes, etc., enough to make up a peerage. Whatever they may be, their accent, conversation, and tone show at once that they have been in the habit of mixing with English gentlemen; yet they were not able to escape the parental command to clear out. Let me say in conclusion that to send to Australia a poor young man without a good trade is to consign him to hopeless drudgery in the centres of civilisation, or to oblivion and death in the vast silent wastes where even the blacks sometimes die for want of water.

Yrs., 'WARAANE',
Sydney

PROTECTION FOR RARE BIRDS

SIR, IT MAY INTEREST SOME of your readers to know that when covert shooting in the East Riding of Yorkshire on 16 January, we had the pleasure of flushing a bittern twice during the day. I am glad to say that the bird was in a locality where both the proprietor and the keeper do their best to preserve any rare stranger that may visit them, the destruction of which one so much regrets seeing recorded almost weekly in your valuable paper, by persons who more often than not wish to appear under the head of naturalists.

Yrs., HENRY S. BOYNTON,
Burton Agnes, Hull

At home in the 'larder'

[It is a pleasure to be able to record the appearance of a rare bird without at the same time having to chronicle its destruction, and it would be well if Sir Henry Boynton's example were more generally followed. Were this the case, there is no doubt that many beautiful and inoffensive birds which used formerly to breed in England, and have become scarce through constant persecution, would once more take up their quarters in this country, and afford pleasure to many who have now no opportunity of observing them. – Ed.]

1893

FROZEN INSECTS

Sir, During the late frost, while moving some stones, we found several caterpillars frozen quite hard. Would not that intense frost kill them off with certainty?

Yrs., GEORGE BOUSFIELD

[No, not certainly, nor even probably. We have placed the larvae of moths in the open, during intense cold, when they have become frozen quite stiff, even to brittleness; and it was easy to break them into pieces as readily as icicles. Other larvae, treated in the same manner but afterwards removed to a warm room, soon recovered, and crawled about without any apparent discomfort from such suspended animation of several days' duration. Intense cold seems to have little effect on insect life, other than indirectly preserving them, for during long frosts the natural enemies of the insects are less destructive than in more open weather. – Ed.]

TICKS ON COWS' UDDERS

Sir, I am sending, as requested by you, one tick taken from the udders of my cattle for identification. It is only after close examination that I am able to detect the insects. If you will give publicity to this in your columns, it may produce valuable information concerning the history of the tick. I think I stated in my former letter that our local vet has never noticed these parasites on cattle. Indirectly I have, like so many others, to thank Miss Ormerod for the discovery, as had I not been dressing the cattle for warble fly, I should not have noticed the ticks.

Yrs., RALPH ARTHUR,
Torybryan Rectory, Newton
Abbot, S. Devon

[The specimen sent is the *Ixodes recinus*. – Ed.]

A CURIOUS SHOT

SIR, WHILE SUPERINTENDING range practice here yesterday a shot was made which strikes me as worth recording. A man was firing at 200 yards lying down, with the Lee-Metford rifle; and, as he fired, one of the common large white kites, swooping down from the barracks some 300 ft. above, crossed the range at a great pace, the high wind favouring him. He crossed about half way between the firing point and the target, and the bullet broke the pinions of both wings, passing through the bird's breast, and got an 'inner' very near the bull's eye. The kite fell without a movement. During 11 years pretty heavy range work I have never known a case similar to the above, though once, in India, I remember a bullet striking the top edge of an iron target, and then hitting a myna that had perched on top of the stop-butt. This was a Martini bullet, and only feathers remained of the bird. Query: if the man firing in the first of the above cases had objected to the record of the 'inner' to him, on the ground that, but for the kite, he would have made a bull, would his objection have been a sound one? Should the officer have cancelled the shot? And, if so, who should have paid for the extra round thus expended.

Yrs., G.F. WHITEHEAD,
(Capt.) 24th Regt, Aden

1894

CURIOUS NEST OF SWALLOW

Sir, A swallow has built its nest on the cogwheel, known as the wallower on the windmill at Corton, near Lowestoft. The wallower in question is about 4 ft. across and the distance of the nest from the centre I put at 1 ft. 2 in. If this be correct and the rate at which the wallower turns when running be an average of 27 revolutions per minute, it follows that the nest must travel at the rate of 180 feet per minute. I was told that the bird, when sitting, usually travelled tail foremost; and generally when entering or leaving the mill she had to make use of the hole through which the laying shaft projected. This made it necessary for her to dodge the sails and of course they were hung pretty close to the wall of the mill. I think that those who know what creaking and shaking go on, even in the fixed portions at the top of a mill, will agree with me that this Corton swallow has chosen a very wonderful place for nesting.

Yrs., RUSSELL J. COLMAN,
Corton, Lowestoft

RUSSIAN BEATERS

Sir, Perhaps a sketch on how we treat our beaters in Russia may amuse brethren of the gun at home. Last week we rose at six o'clock in the dark, with the thermometer 14° Fahrenheit below freezing. After breakfast we drove in sledges 15 versts to the ground, and found assembled there 80 beaters, 34 of whom had walked 18 versts to get there. In several of the beats, the water and slush, when the crust was broken through, was over the knees, and the covert so thick that it was a fight to get through. A large proportion of the beaters were women, and their costumes were frozen as stiff as boards. Many of them wore only birch sandals. When it was over they received the equivalent of 1s. per man, and 10d. per woman, and trotted off to do the 18 versts back again, singing and shouting with glee at being 2d. over the usual fee. The next day they all turned out again to repeat the performance. This they do on a crust of bread and an onion or a piece of salt fish, which they bring with them. Amongst them is an old fellow of nearly 90, who never wears a cap. I have seen him, in 70° of frost, lightly clad and always bareheaded, leading the flank.

Yrs., A.H.B.

1895

RATS

Sir, By a sort of Box and Cox arrangement, I have possession of this house by day and the rats take possession at night. Some 6 months ago they forced an entry, and I reckon that the tax they levy at about 5s. per night. Carpets, clothes, boots – a serious matter in these strike days – anything and everything suited and unsuited to their palate, do they seize on and destroy. The other night they raided my childrens' cupboard, and the poor dolls that had been snugly tucked up for the night by loving hands were found in the morning eyeless and faceless, while the skin of a toy lion was torn off its body. Last night was a typical one. I was aroused at about 3 a.m. by a sort of devil's dance being performed in the bedroom. I lit a candle, and found soon enough that the enemy had been at work. The moment I lay down again and put out the light, back they came and resumed their pranks. Missiles stopped them for only a second or two, but at the sight of the candle they magically disappeared. This game was played for two hours, when I dropped off to sleep, worn out. In the morning I found that the tassel of one blind had been gnawed to pieces, the carpet had been torn away in two places, a mat had been nibbled all along one edge and practically destroyed, and the bottom of the door had been eaten away. The wretches are so bold that I was able to creep up on one in the dark and whack at it with a hairbrush. Of course I only barked my knuckles. Now, what am I to do? I dare not turn in a ferret or use poison. I have tried every conceivable kind of trap and baited them with the most tasty morsels, and my keeper has tried his hand – but all in vain. Cats have been shut up in rooms and taken nothing. If this sort of annoyance lasts much longer I shall have to pack up my traps and make tracks. Will anyone come to my rescue?

Yrs., HOLCOMBE INGLEBY,
Heacham Hall, Norfolk

Sir, Anything is worth trying to get rid of a plague as Mr Holcombe Ingleby describes. The plan I now mention succeeded in one case, and I hope it may do so in his. A professional ratcatcher was called in who caught one rat. This he tarred all over with coal tar, and let go at the entrance of one of their runs. This was all, and no more rats were seen in that house. In H. Ingleby's case I should think two or three rats should be taken and tarred, and, if the rats disappear, the next thing to do is overhaul the drains.

Yrs., Commander GRIFFIN,
R.N., Teignmouth

1896

SPEEDY POLICE

THE POLICE AT NOTTINGHAM have been taking energetic measures to stop the unduly fast riding of bicycles in and about the town. The difficulty of stopping bicyclists who are seen riding at an excessive pace was successfully overcome by the device of having some members of the force who could ride stationed at certain places with their machines, and one of these officers was despatched after any man who rode furiously to obtain his name and address. The only objection we can see to the plan is that the constable must of necessity ride faster than the offender in order to overtake him; but this, in the circumstances, is permissible. It is by such checks as these that furious riding may effectively be dealt with.

1897

FOOTBALL'S SEAMY SIDE

FOR THE MULTITUDE, LOOKING round for its craving for the gladiatorial, the game of football seems to be the nearest approach to what it seeks that is readily and cheaply at hand. There is nothing in the game itself to suggest brutality, except to the vicious mind inclined to brutal things. It is not the conduct of the players, but the attitude of the spectators that has to be complained of. Whilst a number of estimable and gentle-natured people are able to thoroughly enjoy football without suffering any debasement of their natures, it is none the less a remarkable fact that the game has a power of attracting the riff-raff of society which would not be brought together under other conditions. The inhuman practice that is indulged in in the provinces of attacking referees who have umpired a match to the best of their ability, but without meeting the approval of some of the spectators must, if continued, lead to the exercise of repressive measures by the powers of the land. So far our games have not been interfered with by the police, but if the practice of surrounding a defenceless man and attacking him with some fifty fists and boots at a time is persevered with, the law must interfere. It is no longer possible to blink at the fact that a large amount of brutal human scum assembles at football matches in certain parts of the country.

WILD PIGEONS IN AMERICAN FORESTS

NOT SO VERY MANY YEARS ago American woods, at certain seasons and in favoured districts, were full of passenger pigeons. They were to be found in tens of thousands, darkening the air like a cloud, and so thickly did they settle upon the trees that the branches snapped and were broken off by their weight. Men in their greed and thirst for slaughter literally mowed them from off the branches; and no doubt, if breechloaders had been as common in the States in those days as they are at the present time, the work of annihilation would have been more quickly and completely accomplished. It was indeed insensate folly to carry on such wholesale slaughter of these visitors, and thus to exterminate or drive them away. Only 512 pigeons were offered for sale in the markets of San Francisco and Los Angeles, California, during the 5 months of last season; whereas in the same length of time 82,522

Piebald Woodcock (shot in the United States)

teal and 47,565 mallard ducks were received for sale. The State Game Warden of Michigan, Mr C.S. Osborne, in his last biennial report, announced that a few wild pigeons are now to be found in the State, and he is extremely anxious that complete protection and every opportunity should be afforded them to increase in numbers.

1898

THE 55½ LB TAY SALMON

SIR, THE WATER I WAS privileged to fish was a short stretch about 2 miles from Perth, belonging to the Earl of Mansfield, and on the day mentioned I had fished all I knew with the fly until 4.30, never getting a suspicion of a pull. I therefore determined to return for the spinning rod and prawns. A few minutes before 6.00 I made the first cast, and the third found me fast into what I instinctively knew to be a big fish. He was hooked just below Woody Island, and was destined to give me a very exciting time. The reel screeched as he shot down the river, whilst I had to run to try to get opposite to him. A splendid fight commenced, for the fish was as active as a pound trout, and for half an hour never rested a moment until he reached a deep hole, and then occurred the most exciting feature of the run. The line in some way got hitched, broke, and was slipping through the ring when I lowered the point for Mr Campbell to catch the retreating portion. He did so, and as the beast was at the moment quiet, the line only just knotted when he tore across the river, taking out at least 100 yds. of line. This he repeated twice, and you can imagine one's anxiety with such a strain on (literally) a trout reel line with a knot continually passing through the rings. The fish was moving the whole time, otherwise one could never have landed him on such tackle. However, at 7.20 – half a mile below where the fish was hooked – he suddenly caved in, and then again occurred another time of anxious suspense as the rod was bent double in bringing him within reach of Mr Campbell's gaff. There was a spice of romance about the whole scene, as the fish was towed on to the shallows – moonlit water amid some of the finest scenery in Scotland. But the fish had not a kick left, and there he lay surrounded by Perth fishers, and never shall I forget their sportsmanlike conduct, who had followed the run all through, silently and sympathetically, until the 'fush' was on the bank, when I heard a Scotsman remark, 'He's a prood mon the day.' The length of the fish was 50 in., girth 30 in., weight 55½ lb., condition splendid.

Yrs., ALFRED G. GOODWIN,
Junior Army and Navy Club

[This fish was killed with a 14 ft. cane-built, steel-centre, Pennell pattern (Hardy) rod and very fine undressed Manchester Cotton Co.'s line. – Ed.]

THE GERMAN EMPEROR'S 44-POINTER STAG

SIR, I SEND YOU A PICTURE of the much-talked-about head of a red deer killed by the Emperor William on 27 September last in his forest at Rominten. There is nothing extraordinary about its size, for the length along the curve is but 30 in., though it is of wide span, i.e. 44½ in. The extraordinary number of small tine, viz. 22 on the right and 19 on the left antler (constituting what the Germans call an *ungerader* or uneven 44-pointer) makes it one of the most remarkable trophies obtained within the last two centuries, rivalling the 46-pointer shot by Duke Casimir of Coburg, in 1746, and the famous, though much overrated, 66-pointer killed by the Elector Frederick III of Brandenburg, subsequently first King of Prussia, in 1696. As to size, the clean weight of the 1898 'monster', 24 st. 6 lb., is insignificant when compared with the stags of 50 and 60 stone of the seventeenth century.

Yrs., W.A. BAILLIE-GROHMAN,
Schloss Matzen, Tyrol

1899

PECULIARITY IN DRESS

SIR, I HAVE READ YOUR article on the above topic, and must say I think the present system is better than the former. Young men (I had a son recently at Oxford) are freer, and not so much surrounded by conventionality, and, in my humble opinion, more healthy owing to the care they take of themselves after exertion – either rowing, footballing, or cricketing – so much so that, as soon as the game is over, they at once put on a necktie and overcoat, and, as soon as possible, jump into a hot bath. The latter is certainly a good thing, but not as followed as it were by a son of mine at a public school where there were 500 boys. On Saturdays, when they had a hot bath, he considered it most essential to race round the quad, when snow was on the ground, in his nightshirt and bare feet before jumping into bed. This is on the principle of the Russian bath. Wonderful to relate, the young man is in robust health! As regards top hats, they are, in my opinion, an abomination, except when you come an imperial crowner as I did early this season.

Yrs., C.H.

[We scarcely see how the above letter touches on the subject of our leading article. Whether a man dress in the height of fashion or as the veriest sloven, has nothing whatever to do with the care he takes of himself after exercise. At the same time the practice of taking a hot bath after exercise, though common enough, is not to be recommended when the bather has to take a journey home. The hot water opens the pores of the skin, and there is every chance of catching a cold. As most of our readers are aware, a Turkish bath is followed by a washing of cold or tepid water and a period of rest in the cooling room in order that the subject shall not contract a cold. – Ed.]

DESTRUCTION OF EAGLES

SIR, BELIEVING THAT YOUR sympathy is with those who endeavour to preserve the remnants of our most interesting species from the rapacity and reckless waste of collectors and their agents, I send you a letter which reached me a few days ago from a well- known dealer in the provinces. It may, perhaps, tend to put upon their guard some owners and lessees of ground where eagles breed.

I know, from my own observation, that many – I would rather believe the great majority of – proprietors of such ground give instructions to their keepers and stalkers that the eagles are not to be touched; but these orders are not always enforced with sufficient strictness.

The present is a very aggravated example, the destruction of a pair of birds at the commencement of the breeding season being deliberately planned and already half carried out.

Yrs., W.H. ST QUINTIN

[Copy letter inclosed]
Sir, I have just received a fine Scotch golden eagle. Would you care to purchase it (if not sold) either as a skin, £2, or stuffed, £2 10s., or in case £5 5s., glass sides and front? Are you open to buy a live one? I expect any moment to receive a wire saying one has been secured. If so, it could be sent direct to you from Argyllshire, where it would be captured. Price would be reasonable – 40s. to 50s. or so, I expect.

[Copy reply]
Sir, Nothing would induce me to have anything to do with the destruction of a breeding pair of Scotch golden eagles. As regards a newly captured bird which must be trapped and almost certainly injured more or less it could afford no pleasure to anyone to keep it in confinement.

W.H. St Quintin

[If others would follow the example of our correspondent and refuse to encourage dealers in the manner indicated a considerable check would be put upon their nefarious transactions. It is to be feared that keepers too often forget their duty to their employers and are led astray by tempting offers of reward to shoot or trap rare birds on their employers' estate. The penalty for doing this without permission should be either dismissal or a fine in the shape of a reduction in wages and if this were made known, we should soon hear less of the destruction of rare species. – Ed.]

PERSISTENCY OF SITTING BIRD

Sir, Here is a good instance of the closeness with which a blackbird will sit on her nest. We were cutting down a holly this afternoon, and on its falling to the ground a blackbird flew from beneath. On looking among the branches we found its nest with three eggs in it turned upside down. The bird must have sat on them all the time that the digging was going on round the roots and would not leave its nest even when it felt the tree falling. One of the eggs was broken in the fall, and was found to be almost hatched. We did not know that the nest was there, or else the tree would have been left until all the birds were fledged.

Yrs., R.M.G.

[This brings to mind the case mentioned by Gilbert White of the raven, which sat so close on her nest in an aged oak, that when the tree was doomed to be cut down and at length fell, the raven fell with it and was killed. – Ed.]

1900

HAMMOCKS

SIR, MOST PEOPLE know that a hammock is the only method, except that of Shank's mare, of travelling in West Africa; but, for those who do not, I will briefly describe this, to me, most unpleasant of all conveyances. It consists of a stout pole at least 10 ft. long, to each end of which is fixed a crosspiece of narrow board about 4 ft. in length. These rest on the heads of the four bearers, who walk at either end of them, protecting their heads by a sort of turban or pad stuffed with grass. On the pole is fixed a light oblong frame of wood, covered with American oil cloth, or some other waterproof material, to protect the rider from sun or rain; and from either end of the pole hangs a plaited grass hammock. There also hangs from near the centre of the pole an article not unlike a child's swing, for use as a stirrup or footrest. The rider either reclines or else sits up in the hammock, allowing his feet to dangle in the stirrup, both equally uncomfortable. It is quite the least convenient of all the conveyances I have tried, and a crowded third class carriage on a suburban line, even if that line be the South-Eastern, is a paradise to it. One does not cover much more than three miles an hour; one is in a constant atmosphere of *bouquet d'Afrique* from the perspiring hammock boys; if one has a companion in misfortune one is unable to converse with him, as the narrow roads prevent two

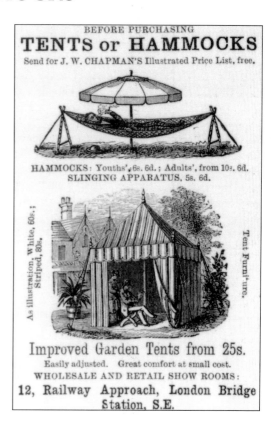

hammocks from travelling abreast; and, after enduring the peculiar jolting for a time one experiences just the same feeling that one feels on landing from a ship after a rough passage.

Yrs., A.R. LOSCOMBE

SELF-DEFENCE FOR BICYCLISTS

SIR, THE OTHER DAY I WAS informed by a lady of my acquaintance that, bicycling about sunset along the towing path from Hampton Court to Kingston, she and a friend were much annoyed by a couple of particularly ill-conditioned cads also riding bicycles. They hung about their back wheels, and pursued them with a running fire of vulgarities. Eventually my friends with their unwelcome escort, overtook another party of bicyclists whereupon the two cads discreetly put down their heads and scorched off. I told the lady that her proper course under the circumstances was to sit up suddenly with all her power of backpedalling and braking, whereupon her persecutor would have bumped her back wheel and almost inevitably come a bad cropper. To anyone acquainted with bicycle racing it is axiomatic that the result of a bump is to send the bumper to swift destruction, the person bumped escaping uninjured.

To get past a menacing tramp, ride point-blank at the aggressor, and at the last moment throw the whole weight of the body to the right or left, as the case may be, thus making a rapid tack. Not one man in a hundred will stand up to a bicycle approaching at speed; the instinct to shrink back, specially in a person unprepared for such a manoeuvre, is irresistible, and according as he steps to the right or left, so the bicyclist swerves swiftly in the opposite direction.

Another point worthy of consideration is the utilisation of the momentum of the bicycle in disabling an opponent. Most of us have at some time or other ventured a passing stroke at the head of a cap-throwing boy, and been surprised how overpowering to him is the result of a forward blow, and how ludicrously inadequate is the effect of a backhander. To bring into subjection this blind force should not be difficult. Of course the reaction from a hard blow dealt at a sturdy tramp might be disastrous to the bicyclist; but, by swerving and so throwing the balance of the machine well to the side of the person to be demolished, the recoil from the shock might be made to run concurrently with the natural recovery from the inclined position in which the blow was delivered.

Another useful way to deal with an assailant is to ride at his side, and, throwing your arms around his neck, to leap on to him, leaving the bicycle to take its chance. The odds are that you, with your momentum, will overbear him and fall on him heavily, while the bicycle relieved of your weight, has a reasonable chance of emerging unharmed. This is a far more desperate plan than the last mentioned and one to be employed only upon very narrow roads, but it ought to give a very great advantage to the bicyclist. Otherwise your adversary can choose the psychological moment for putting his stick into your spokes. By closing with him you take the initiative and the choice of moment rests with you.

Yrs., H. GRAVES

COTTAGE GARDENS

THERE ARE STILL VILLAGE or roadside gardens with great bushes of Daphne and old garden roses with lines of sweet white pinks or pansies, and great masses of crimson, clove, and other carnations, edgings of 'rabbits' ears' or auriculas, or old double primroses, China roses, jasmine or honeysuckles over the rustic porch of larch poles, and rosemary, lavender, and lad's love or other sweet herbs near the bee stands or under the lee of the woodsheds, or closely clustered up beside the cottage door. It is far better to have a well-kept garden full of all the sweetest and most abundant of hardy flowers in bold groups, such as roses, lilies, tulips, daffodils, snowdrops, crocuses, violets, pansies, wall flowers and stocks, delphiniums, lupins, asters, and sun flowers, than to grow scraps of a thousand things or varieties jumbled together. Grow plenty of climbing plants; let there be tea and other roses, clematis, and honeysuckle on walls, arches, or pagodas; and beneath the windows and round the house rosemary, lavender and thyme, musk, mignonette, violets, night-scented stocks, myrtles, with borders for the bees of fragrant thyme.

1905

TRAFFIC CENSUS

SOME VERY INSTRUCTIVE figures of traffic on the Bath Road through Hounslow have been obtained by Mr S.F. Edge. In the 12 hours from 9 am to 9 pm on 2 July, the passage of vehicles to and fro was carefully recorded, with the following result: bicycles 4,577, motor vehicles 577; electric tramcars 407, horse vehicles 209. Total, 5,770. This table shows how greatly the motor car traffic exceeds that of horse-drawn conveyances, and if the roads are made with a view to consulting the needs of those who use them most, obviously the motorist has the greatest claim. But beyond this is the striking preponderance of mechanical traffic. Depend upon it, before very long traffic outside towns, at any rate, and most probably in them also, will be almost entirely mechanical.

1909

GREY SQUIRREL AT MOLESEY

SIR, ONE DAY LAST WEEK I was watching a pair of kingfishers from a wooden foot-bridge which crosses the river Mole about a mile from its junction with the Thames at Hampton Court Bridge, when I saw what I took to be a large, light-coloured rat disporting itself amidst the fallen leaves of a shrubbery. Between me and the animal were some palings, three inches or four inches apart, which did not allow much of a clear view, but after waiting 10 minutes – in a very bad light – I discovered that what I had taken for a rat was a grey squirrel. As I have never seen a grey squirrel at liberty in England before I should much like to know how its presence may be accounted for.

Yrs., 'INQUIRER'

[In 1890, we were presented with an American grey squirrel, one of a consignment of half a dozen. The others were turned out into Bushy Park, about a mile from where our correspondent lately saw the animal above described. And it is not improbable that it may have been a descendant of those which were imported; if so, it is curious that in so long an interval as that which has elapsed since their arrival no report has reached us of any grey squirrel being seen in the district referred to. – Ed.]

GOLDCREST ON WATER

SIR, I WAS WALKING ROUND our small ornamental lake, when my attention was drawn to a movement in the water about 4 or 5 ft. from the bank. I, at first, thought it must be a fish stirring; but as I drew nearer I saw that it was some creature swimming, probably a mouse. It duly reached the land, when, to my astonishment, I saw it was a golden-crested wren; which, after a few moments paused on a tuft of dead grass, flew off into the bushes. I may add that there were several birch leaves on the surface of the water on one of which it might have settled before starting to swim for the shore.

Yrs., E.R. BLAND,
Inglethorpe Manor, Wisbeach

UNPLEASANT INCIDENT

SIR, THE FOLLOWING INCIDENT, which took place today in this village, may possibly serve to explain why foxhunting is in danger of losing the sympathy of village folk. A funeral procession, of which I was one, was on its way to the village cemetery, when a follower of the Oakley Hounds appeared on the scene and began questioning two girls, whose cart was standing by the side of the road in order to allow the bearers to pass. After many loud enquiries as to the whereabouts of the hounds, and how far he was behind them, he spurred up his horse and galloped past the procession, bespattering us all with mud from his horse hooves. For sheer rudeness and absolute disregard for people's feelings, I have never seen anything to equal his behaviour. If such cads hunt they will very quickly stifle all the sympathy and goodwill with which villagers regard a sport always associated in their minds with gentlemen.

Yrs., C.B. HULTON,
Rector of Turvey, Beds.

LUXURIES AND REFINEMENT

IN A WAY, THE PERFECTION of the modern motor car is a thing to be regretted. The public nowadays take things as a matter of course, neither realising the vast difference between motoring as it is today and as it was 6 or 8 years back, not appreciating recent improvements. To them, if they think of it at all, the early cars, with their ungainly appearance, imperfect mechanism and general uncomfortableness, are merely objects of historical interest, as far removed from modern types as 'Puffing Billy' is from a railway locomotive of today. The majority of people, it must be confessed, have taken up the automobile when it was well nigh perfect and hence have come to regard it mainly as a means of getting about, and as devoid of interest or individuality as a Hansom cab. Yet this is rather a matter for regret than otherwise, for a motor car is a complex organism, and needs understanding and humouring to a high degree.

In no way can one get a better idea of the vast improvement recently made in motorcars than by examining the lamps. Headlights are now made, for instance, which throw powerful beams a long distance ahead, can be diverted to shine around corners or even used to read directions on signposts. Lamps that can be trusted not to go out, that will not flicker, die away, or blur the lense; lamps that will burn brightly for hours without attention; lamps that will not scatter oil or diffuse unpleasant odours in their neighbourhood – these are some of the blessings we enjoy today. And should the passengers desire to while away the hours of darkness, a touch will illuminate a car's interior so that they can read or work instead of sitting inactive.

Engines can now be started automat-

MOTORING COMFORT

The Motoluxe is the ideal Motor Rug. Light as a feather and warm as a blanket, its soft fleecy texture keeps out the cold, but is never oppressively heavy.

EVERY bit of it pure alpaca wool—warm, cosy and capable of standing any amount of hard wear. For the closed saloon or the open tourer a Motoluxe Rug is an essential part of winter equipment.

Price
£5 5 0

Foot Muffs to match **39/6**

For OPEN CARS buy the interlined WINDPROOF RUG 10/6 extra.

Insist on the name and ask to see the "Foot Muffs that Match."

Miss Evelyn Laye
and a......

MOTOLUXE

THE SNUGGEST *of* RUGS

OF ALL LEADING STORES EVERYWHERE.

Aldwych.

ically, tyres pumped up without manual labour, lights toned down to prevent dazzle, and flashed into brilliance again in the open country. Does a driver desire to turn to one side or to reverse, he need no longer crane his neck at an awkward angle or call upon his passengers to assist, indicators and a reflector telling him and others all that is required. Ingenious tools can make intricate operations easy, save time, overcome difficulties and generally so alter things as to make it impossible to appreciate what driving a car meant in the early days.

1910

THE LATE KING

NO MORE SALIENT ILLUSTRATION of the relations between King Edward and his subjects at large ever occurred than when, at the Derby last year, he hurried offhand and untended by escort to lead in his victorious colt, plunging into the mob of all sorts and conditions of men that instantly throngs from under the rails and from inclosures when a race is over. Spontaneously the monarch seemed to assume that he was as safe among that medley as if at his own dinner table; and with simultaneous spontaneous sentiment straightaway the throng struck up the National Anthem.

THE LIGHTING OF COUNTRY HOUSES

SIR, THE FOLLOWING EXPERIENCE may be of interest to the owners of country houses who use acetylene gas, or propose to do so as an illuminant. Not long since I had the offices here lighted with acetylene, the installation being fitted with the greatest care. The other night, however, the gas house blew up with a deafening crash that can be likened only to the gun of a Dreadnought; at the same time, all lights were blown out, even lamps and candles, the pictures flapped on walls, window glass descended in showers, and the acetylene house and all near it, including doors, window frames etc., were shivered into fragments, blocks of stone of from 1 ft. to 2 ft. square being hurled in all directions. The shock of the explosion was felt at a distance of three miles, and at a village a mile away the people came out of their houses, judging it was an earthquake. Now all this was caused by quite a small installation, supplying only thirty lights in the offices, chiefly fitted as an experiment before applying the light by means of a much larger installation to the house generally.

I need hardly say that the explosion was, as a matter of course, said by the experts representing this form of lighting to have been caused by the attendant entering the gas house with a naked light. They would naturally not like to admit any other explanation. However, one thing is absolutely certain, and that is that the poor fellow who was so injured had no light of any kind with him. His pipe and his box of matches were next day found in the pocket of his overcoat which he had left in a room 50 yards from the gas house, and he had no

lantern or candle. What happened was this: As the attendant was passing the gas house on his way home he thought he detected an unusual smell, which caused him to slightly open the door, more from curiosity than anything else. The same instant the explosion occurred, and he was picked up insensible 10 yards away, a marvellous escape, although dreadfully injured, if he had entered the gas house he must have been blown to atoms.

Since all this occurred I have heard of numerous casualties from acetylene – some, like mine, apparently for no reason. The only possible cause in my case – and, strange as it seem, similar instances I now

hear have occurred in other places – may be the fact that there was an escape of gas owing to a defective pipe, and that there was also an exceedingly wet and dense fog. The heavy saturated atmosphere and the concentrated fumes of the gas meeting when the door was opened may have caused the catastrophe.

I have often been told by interested persons that acetylene is so safe, because any escape in a house can be detected by its strong smell. Let no one be led away by this theory! If, for instance, a room has been shut up for a few days and the gas has escaped therein, through a rat or mouse perhaps gnawing the little thin lead pipe hidden under the floor, or from several other causes which might occur to injure the great lengths of pipe in one spot or another, then all that is required is a housemaid with a candle, and up she goes and half your house too!

I would warn anyone who fits acetylene gas to, above all, insist that no piping is carried through any cupboards or store-rooms, as a short cut to some other part of the house. Such a place being more or less airtight and unventilated, any escape of the gas is shut in and ready for instant explosion directly the door is opened by a person holding a light, as happened the other day, with terrible effect, in the case of a linen cupboard. I write this merely in the hope of saving future accidents, and I am of the opinion that the use of acetylene generally in country houses is a dangerous illuminant until it is made more 'fool proof', though in my accident there was no suggestion of this kind.

Yrs., RALPH PAYNE-GALLWEY,
Thirkleby Park, Thirsk

ELEPHANT SHOOTING: WHERE TO AIM

SIR, BEING INTERESTED IN this question, I took the opportunity when an elephant had become dangerous at a continental circus yesterday and had to be shot, to make experiments. A well-known explorer and elephant shot and a professional elephant hunter kindly lent me their rifles, and I also had one of my own, these gentlemen being present and instructing me where to aim. The elephant was an Indian female, about 20 years old. She was tied in a building, so I could not use the regular steel-pointed bullets for the elephant rifles for fear of ricochets, but used soft-nosed bullets. Shooting at ten yards' distance, the

elephant being broadside on, I fired two shots with my double 400 Purdey cordite rifle and hollow pointed bullet, taking the ear shot. The first shot I aimed at a point 1 in. horizontally behind the left earhole. This shot partly stunned the elephant which slightly swayed but did not fall, but she made no attempt to get loose or turn on me. The second barrel fired almost immediately afterwards and aimed at the earhole, struck it. This immediately brought her down and, according to a veterinary whom I had brought with me, killed her. But as she still showed signs of life, I took one of the elephant rifles, a single (I do not know the bore, but can obtain the information), and gave her, by directions, several shots at various parts of the shoulder. She partly rose at the first of these shots, but then fell, and lay merely breathing. I then went in front of her and put three or four shots with the third rifle, an 11½ millimetre weapon (.450 bore) which was very light and kicked very hard, putting the shots one above the other about 2 in. apart, vertically from between the eyes up to the base of the trunk, her head being on a level with me. According to the veterinary, my second shot fired almost immediately after the first (which so stunned her that she was practically without feeling) killed her. The remaining shots were unnecessary, and there was no cruelty in firing them as she was unconscious, though breathing. I enjoined the veterinary to make very careful notes of the locality, direction, depth of penetration, and effect of each shot; but I had to leave to catch a train before the post-mortem was made.

Yrs., WALTER WINANS

Sir, I enclose the veterinary report of the shot elephant. The bullets show, to my mind, that it was one of the little Purdey rifle bullets which went into the heart cavity. The

Mr George Grey who was so badly mauled by a lion near Nairobi that he died a few days later, is seen in the above picture seated in one of the patent folding boats of the Accordian Boat Company, to whose kindness we are indebted for the photograph.

shooting seems to show that with a soft-nosed bullet the head shot is useless even with heavy elephant rifles at a few feet distance. Also the fact that the elephant had brain fever is interesting as showing why elephants turn nasty at times.

'Of all the bullets that have got into the skull from the ear side or in front none has hurt the brain pan or the brain. The bullets from the ear side as well as in front have not advanced into the true brain pan more than 2 cms. (¾ in. roughly). The hit parts of the skull have been entirely broken up. Some bullets have rebounded from the second upper jaw grinder of the left side, and have broken up the left lower jaw branch. The left exterior auditory passage was not hurt. Of the brain bullets, only splinters have been found. Of all bullets directed into the left side of the breast (region of the heart) the greater part went too high. Only two bullets went through the ventricles (*herz vorkammern*), and in consequence of these wounds the heart has bled to death in

the pericardium, and in the same time in the left diaphragm sack. Both bullets have been found in the coagulated blood (nine tenths of which were leucocytes) in the free room of the pericardium. It is interesting to note that when inspecting the brain it was found that the animal was suffering from the beginnings of brain fever. There were larger parts of the left large brain hemisphere and of the left small brain moiety on the base in a stage of bloody inflammation (intensive cherry coloured) under the pia mater and intensive injection of the blood vessels.'

CARTHORSE ATTACKING FOX

SIR, WHEN STAYING RECENTLY in Sussex with my brother-in-law, Mr Arthur Lawrence, I saw a most curious instance of the sympathy which sometimes exists between the larger animals and birds. In a field of about 10 acres there was a small pond about an acre in extent, on which were some ornamental waterfowl belonging to my brother-in-law. In the next field was a four-year-old carthorse. These fields being in sight of the house, we were astonished one day to hear much commotion at the pond, and saw a fox making off with one of the ducks. Before we had time to leave our breakfast and get to the spot to render assistance the horse from the next field, attracted no doubt by the noise made by the waterfowl, suddenly appeared and, to our astonishment, not only caused the fox to relinquish his hold on the bird, but, seizing him in his teeth, held him in the water for some time, releasing him only on our arrival. I may add that in getting into the field the carthorse jumped some oak rails 4 ft. 6 in. high, breaking the top bar, as might be expected. That foxes will attack large birds, I have found by sad experience, for on one occasion a tame emu of mine was severely injured by two foxes that suddenly attacked it; but, being a powerful bird, it eventually escaped from them.

Yrs., GEORGE R. BURTENSHAW, Clewer, nr. Windsor

THE SIZE AND WEIGHT OF GOLF BALLS

SIR, ONE OF THE GREATEST objections to the small and heavy balls now in use is that they have made it far easier for any kind of hit to travel against the wind. They have to a considerable extent taken away the right and proper advantage previously held by the man who could play one of the finest and most scientific of all shots, the wind cheater. When the heavy balls were first brought out they had the characteristic of not travelling so well as other rubber-cored balls when not quite properly hit, but now the manufacturers have 'improved' this 'defect' away. Whatever may be the diffi- culties in laying down and enforcing the regulations for a complete standardisation of the ball – and they have undoubtedly been much exaggerated – there can be none to be faced in establishing by rule a definite size and weight. The latter should be insufficient to make the ball sink in water.

Yrs., 'A LONDON GOLFER'

HORNETS' NEST IN TUSK OF LIVING ELEPHANT

SIR, ON 5 MAY LAST, near a place called Killegui in French Guinea, I came across a bull, cow and calf elephant. Before I could fire the bull went off, and led me round a circle of about 7 miles. When I got up to him and killed him we were about a mile from where I first saw the three. This bull had only one whole tusk, which weighed 48½ lb.; the other tusk was rotten and hollow and had a hornets' nest inside of it. I actually saw the hornets crawling in and out of the tusk when I got alongside of him.

I should like to know if this is a unique case, or if you or any of your readers have heard of a similar case before. I don't think the elephant was in any pain, as at the base of the tusk there was bony matter a couple of inches thick. I am preserving this tusk as a momento, for, of course, it is of no value as ivory.

Yrs., F. St G. TUCKER,
Sierra Leone

INDIAN CHUTNEY

SIR, CAN ANY READER kindly inform me whether the manufacturers of Rustomjee Dadabhoy Motiwalla, No 1, Marine Lane Fort, Bombay, can be procured in London? and more pre-eminently his Green Mango Chutney?

Yrs., 'DINICK'

KINGFISHER IN THE HOUSE

SIR, LADY PEMBROKE THINKS the fact that she discovered a kingfisher in her sitting-room on 1 October is of sufficient interest to be recorded among your notes on Natural History.

Yrs., R.T. ATTHILL,
Wilton House, Salisbury

PHEASANT AND PIKE

SIR, WHEN WE WERE SHOOTING in Co. Down on 4 November 1911, a somewhat curious incident occurred. A hen pheasant was shot by one of the party and fell in some open water in the centre of a small marsh, where it could be plainly discerned. While a keeper was approaching with a retriever the pheasant was seen to disappear beneath the surface, being evidently drawn down by a mysterious agency. For some time two dogs searched in vain. The depth of the water was such as to make it just necessary for them to swim. Suddenly, after one of the dogs passed over the exact spot where the pheasant had disappeared, the bird again rose to the surface. Both dogs appeared most reluctant to touch it. Finally it was brought to land, when it was perceived that the neck and crop had been torn open. The time elapsed from the bird falling until it re-appeared was fully 15 minutes. The only conceivable explanation would appear to be that the bird was seized by a pike, and, in spite of the well-known voracity of these fish, such an experience would seem well-nigh unique.

Yrs., G.S. READE,
Firgrove, Muckamore,
Co. Antrim

[Somewhat similar experiences are not unknown. A big pike certainly does not draw the line at feather or fur, but a pheasant must be rather a mouthful for him. In *The Field* of 11 January 1908, Dr Bolton McCausland described a case in which the pheasant was not only seized, but apparently swallowed by a pike. – Ed.]

1912

THE VOICE OF THE GIRAFFE

Sir, I HAVE HAD CHARGE OF many giraffes for varying periods, and only from one of them did I ever hear any vocal sound. This was an old female who sometimes, but very rarely (I think on not more than two or three occasions) uttered a husky grunting sound if I tantalised her by holding a bit of green stuff just out of her reach. It might perhaps have been audible at 20 yards distance, and was something like the 'begging' noise made by very hungry or thirsty donkeys when one approaches them with food or water after a long trek.

Yrs., A.L. BUTLER,
Superintendent of Game
Preservation, Sudan
Government, Khartoum

MOTOR CARS AND FOXHOUNDS

Sir, WITH A VIEW TO PREVENT the repetition of an accident similar to that which befell the Duke of Rutland's hounds on Friday evening in last week, may I, through your columns, appeal to all country motorists to light their head lamps, even on clear moonlit nights? The glare of a headlight, even on a winding road, is visible at a great distance, and thus enables the huntsman to give due notice of the presence of hounds by blowing his horn, and to otherwise take measures for the safety of the pack. In the case alluded to a motor car with no headlight (the driver subsequently explaining that he did not think one necessary as the night was clear and moonlit) rounded a corner about 300 yards ahead of the hounds. The driver failed to hear the huntsman's horn, could not see the hounds, and dashed right through them, killing one, maiming another and inflicting minor injuries on five couple more.

Yrs., ROBERT MANNERS,
F.M.

PLOVER SHOT FROM A MOTOR CAR

SIR, AN OWNER OF A MOTOR car in this neighbourhood, who is his own chauffeur, tried the last week in January to see if green plover could be shot from the car. On the first day he and one passenger shot from the car 15 plover, and on the second day three guns shot 38. Some of the birds were shot flying and others standing on the ground, when the speedometer marked 20 miles per hour. The guns were all choked, and all three of the shooters assured me that they made no allowance, but shot straight at the birds. The car travelled 75 miles in two days.

Mr Henry Watts says: 'If the face is allowed to leave the stock so that both eyes can see the object there will probably be trouble.' Yes, to the large majority of shooters who think that they shoot by placing the sight 'fair on the centre of the object aimed at'. The charge cannot be centred on the mark if the shooter sees his gun at the instant the trigger is pressed. He must keep the stock clear of his shoulder, see the mark, and think of the mark. The instant he sees or thinks of his gun he ceases to see the mark. He cannot make an allowance off the mark without thinking of his gun; therefore it is impossible to 'lead' a bird.

Yrs., 'CONTORTIONIST'

THE CATAPAULT

SIR, I HAVE FOUND THE catapault a most useful weapon for collecting small birds, and have still in my possession one which I made 38 years since. This has from time to time been remade up in its original style, but it is not now quite the same as it used to be, the quality of modern elastic comparing badly with that of 25 or 30 years ago. The catapault figured in the accompanying illustration represents my old weapon. The fork I cut from a hazel bush in 1874.

As regards the load, it depends entirely on the size of the quarry. For all round shooting there is nothing to equal a single buck shot 13 to the ounce, which will kill any bird as big as a lapwing up to 50 or 60 yards. For smaller birds, such as finches at 20 or 30 yards range, 3 pellets of No. 1 shot is a capital charge if placed closely together in a triangle in the pouch. For long distance shots bullets of ½ in. diameter and round pellets the size of marbles hit with tremendous force up to about 150 yards, and will go clean through a bird as big as a dove at closer range. I have still in my possession the skins of squirrels and rats. A rat which I shot 30 years ago, dropped dead at about 30 yards' range while running between a couple of corn stacks. I used a single buck which struck it over the left eye, passed through the head, down the neck, and through the left shoulder, and lodged under the skin behind it. At another time, using a small, round stone, I killed a nightjar while it was flying rapidly along at about 25 or 30 yards' range. On picking it up I found that the stone had gone in one side of the breast and out the other. With a single buck shot, I dropped a lapwing at 54 yards, which was flying between 40 and 50 yards high and going quickly. On another occasion, wanting some goldcrest skins, by using a pinch of No. 6 shot each time, I got six of these little birds within half an hour from tall pine trees. I merely mention these few instances to give some idea of what the same catapult properly made, using different charges, is capable of doing. The notches on this old weapon, numbering about 200

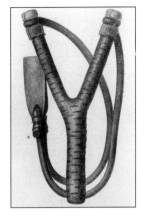

in all, I used to cut to indicate each bird gathered in its early days.

As regards marksmanship, it is surprising, when one is in constant practice, what remarkable shooting may be achieved with the catapult. We, as boys, between 30 and 40 years ago, used to stick up pennies in the ground and, with a single B.B. pellet at about 15 yards try our skill. If we missed three out of six it was bad shooting.

Yrs., F.W. FROHAWK

TO CATCH RATS INSIDE A HOUSE

Sir, Set an ordinary gin with a square slab of cheese placed under a fold of a newspaper, cut a square in the single fold of the newspaper to fit the size of the cheese. The cheese only will be seen protruding from the paper, and it is extraordinary how the older rats are taken in. I have caught as many as 16 in four nights between dinner and bedtime, taking care to remove the rat directly it is caught. The best way to cut the paper is to pencil the size of the cheese on the paper before tying it to the gin, and then tie with string so as to cut down the cheese till it gets to the rind, and is concealed. When the gin is set under the paper the edges can be folded so as to hide the contents.

Yrs., W.I. HADDEN,
Braunton, Devon

SPARROW HAWK KILLED BY HEN

Sir, Last week a chicken, one of a brood of eight, disappeared from the stable yard of Holesday House, Lynton, much to the distress of the lodgekeeper who had charge of the brood. The following day, hearing the hen making a great noise and evidently very angry, she rushed from the lodge to see what was the cause, and found the hen standing over a sparrow hawk, which gave one or two convulsive twitches and then lay dead. The hen had her wings out-stretched, and a leg each side of the hawk; she was not pecking at it but making a great outcry. I have lived in the country all my life, but this is the first time I have heard of a hen killing a hawk. I know they will drive them away, often flying 10 ft. or 20 ft. into the air in so doing; but I should be glad to know if such cases have been recorded before, or are common. I examined the hawk, but found no marks on her, and the plumage was very little disturbed.

Yrs., F.B.E.

[We have known several cases of hawks being attacked and killed by poultry. – Ed.]

1917

THE SPIRIT THAT DENIES

THE LEADERS OF GERMANY are even more wicked than the dregs of the population. A nation has the rulers it deserves and chooses to obey and Germans of every class have not only welcomed the orders given but have applauded those that have carried them out. The barbarous spirit of a brutal ferocity is in their blood and even their women showed it at the very beginning of the war. Some of our prisoners – alas, too few! – have returned from the hell in which they were confined. They will tell you how German Red Cross nurses gibed at the British wounded, taunted them with refusals of the food and drink they needed and even deliberately added to the pains of helpless men. It is a repulsive subject on which we will not linger for we are willing to believe in this case at any rate that these fiends in woman's form may have been overexcited by an hysterical passion they could not overcome. But what other nation could have produced them? And in what other nation could the sacred symbol of the Red Cross be so abused, not on the battle field alone but even within its own borders? The brutal destruction of hospital ships is but another example of the same defiance of all humanity, as is the constant shelling of every ambulance station at the Front which has been the beastly habit of the Boche for years and, if they pay so little heed to any of the sanctities of life, what wonder is it that they have no reverence whatever for the dead? The hideous story of the use to which they turn their corpses is the fitting climax to a theory of war which would disgrace a cannibal. In every other war, in every other land, the soldier who dies fighting for his country is at least sure that what slight rites be possible on active service will be extended to his body after death. The German soldier has no such assurance. After he has been hurled into the furnace of shellfire and he has suffered the final agony of a lacerating wound, he is collected (it appears), bound up in bundles and melted into glycerine and pigs' food which brings in a handsome profit.

1918

CURIOUS CONDUCT OF A HEN

SIR, ABOUT 4 WEEKS AGO, one of my rabbit-catchers took ten sheldrake's eggs, which he found in a rabbit-hole on an island on Loch Leven, and put them under a hen. Eight of them hatched out, but when they were about 3 weeks old the hen disappeared and could not be found for several hours. In the evening she turned up with 14 young partridges which she had annexed. She mothered the ducks as well as the partridges, but did not like the ducks and six of them died. She now has a family of two ducks and 12 partridges which she is bringing up. I have never heard of a similar case.

Yrs., BASIL MONTGOMERY,
Kinross, N.B.

THROWING THE CRICKET BALL

SIR, BEFORE GOING TO Uppingham, I was at school with the boy who accomplished what, I believe, is still looked upon as a record throw for a boy of his age, if not for a boy of any age while still at school. Leamington College in the 'seventies and 'eighties, under Dr Joseph Wood (late head of Harrow), was included amongst the forty great English public schools. A Major Edlman, who resided at Leamington, sent all his eight sons there, and seven were at the school all at the same time (surely another record?). It was Edlman sixtus who, in his sixteenth year, threw a cricket ball a few inches over 116 yards in the college sports. I think this happened in 1883 or 1884. All the family were more or less good at games. Edlman major, who went out to Africa to farm ostriches; minor, known as 'Dick', who became a Bank of England clerk, tertius, quartus, and sixtus (another 'Dick') were all first-rate cricketers, and could throw a ball further than the majority of schoolboy throwers. They all, I remember, had tremendously long arms, and Edlman sextus started throwing at a very early age. He was the best (I should really say worst) thrower of a stone I ever knew up to the time he was about 13 years old. I scarcely ever met him on his way to school without his having a stone to throw, and on several occasions saw him pursued by a 'Peeler' either for throwing stones or ringing the bells in Clarendon-square. He was a very good all-round athlete, but I have never heard anything of him for over thirty years.

Yrs., GEORGE A. FOTHERGILL

Sir, It may not be generally known in this country how far George Washington's stone (one authority states that it was a silver dollar) flew when he flung it across the Rappahannock about 170 years ago (he was 16 years old at the time). I wrote to the postmaster of the village where this took place, and he replied that in Washington's youth that particular stretch of the Rappahannock was supposed to be 125 yards in width. My letter to the postmaster above referred to was written ten years ago, and I write now with his reply before me. Prob-ably George Washington could have thrown a cricket ball much further than a stone, say 150 yards.

Yrs., HUBERT SATCHWELL

[Everybody knows the story of the Englishman who, on visiting the Rappahannock and hearing the account of Washington's throw, replied 'Oh, I'm not in the least surprised at that, for a dollar went ever so much further in those days than it does now.' – Ed.]

A LETTER FROM SPAIN

MUCH RESPECTED SIR, Please excuse my writing this letter to you. I am a peace loving, simple worker in the wool trade and full of wholehearted enthusiasm with the struggles of the war; I feel always compelled to stand up for my martyr brothers, the French, the Italian, the English and their other Allies who shed their blood to bring about a state of freedom never seen before however much desired.

I am greatly desirous of reading your propaganda documents, and – so as not to be obliged to keep on bothering those who lend them to me – I should like very much – if this does not cause you trouble or loss – to be favoured with these documents in order to have them always to hand and to be able to study them in our hours of leisure in the company of our fellow workmen that they may bring courage and valour to our minds. For we look at and study again and again as much the photographs as the articles contained in these reviews – The Demons of the Sea – The German Terrorism – The War in April, 1918 – The Photographs of the British Womens' Work in Wartime – The Outline of the German Ambitions. Of this I would like to make a picture – so as to keep as a souvenir.

Without anything else to say, I trust you will excuse my bothering you. I am always your humble servant, and conclude with 'Long live the Republic, the Allies, France, Italy, England, and their brother Allies!'

Yrs., JOSÉ RUBIRA,
Valls

[We have sent the original of which this is a translation to our Ministry of Information, and we feel sure our propaganda officials will be touched by the appeal and send out all our correspondent's needs. – Ed.]

1919

ST ANDREWS COLLEGE, GRAHAMSTOWN, SOUTH AFRICA

ABOUT 1,000 OLD ANDREANS served during the war. The average number of boys in the school for the past ten years has been 210. There is no conscription in S. Africa, and all service is voluntary. Casualties: Killed or died of wounds 118, wounded 200, missing 3, prisoners 29 (now repatriated).

Honours: V.C. 2, D.S.O. 13, C.M.G. 1, D.C.M. 7, M.M. 2, M.C. 41, bar to M.C. 5, D.F.C. 4, D.S.C. 1, Italian medal for valour 2, Croix de Guerre 3, Legion of Honour 1, Russian St George's Cross 1, Order de Léopold 1. There were 120 commissions held by Andreans.

WILD GOOSE SHOOT

SIR, THE FOLLOWING RECORD OF wild goose shooting, in one day, by a single sportsman with a shoulder gun (12 bore) may be of interest. The Marquis de Campo Real, shooting on the Marismas del Guadalquivir at a place called 'Las Nueras' in December 1916, bagged to his own gun 95 greylags. He began at daybreak and shot them flighting over decoys until 10 o'clock. He then went home for breakfast and returned at 11.30 when he continued shooting until 1.30 and then knocked off. He tells me that had he been placed at a small pool some 80 yds. further than where he was he would have killed many more.

Yrs., C. H. DE AMÉZAGA,
Madrid

KNIFE WITH A HISTORY

SIR, THIS KNIFE HAD BEEN used on board the Norwegian S.S. Faedrelaudet to cut the pages of two books when the vessel was about 140 nautical miles N.E. of Hull, bound for Cronstadt; an unexpected wave caused the user of the knife to leave his deck chair and take shelter in the cabin. It is believed that the knife was then dropped on the deck and that the wave swept it through a scupper hole. This happened on 6 August 1898, and the knife was not seen again until May, 1911, that is an interval of 12¾ years; it was then found embedded in the flesh of a silver hake which was being decapitated in Manchester Fish Market. The fish from which the knife was recovered was one of a consignment landed at Fleetwood. The knife, which was lost on the eastern side of England, was recovered from the Irish Sea. Mr Mason had held a responsible position in H.M. service in Manchester, and as his name was on the knife there was no difficulty in tracing him when the find was announced in the Manchester newspapers. The knife is not corroded, it has not been cleaned or oiled. Yet, all its four blades open easily, and

Knife recovered after twelve years inside a hake

close with a 'snap' like that of a new knife; the absence of rust indicates that the knife was snatched as it was descending to the ocean bed, and that the oil of the fish's body kept it clean.

Yrs., 'NORTHERNER'

CURIOUS BEHAVIOUR OF A DIVER

SIR, ON 10 MAY I WAS walking round a small loch in Sutherland with a friend, he on one side, I on another. Red-throated divers were on the water. One, apparently startled by my friend, commenced to fly, but while still over the water, suddenly came down at a sharp angle, landed on his breast, ricochetted about 5 yards along and 4 feet in the air, and landed on his side, when he at once dived and joined his mate. After half a minute's interval, he again rose out of the water and flew straight

towards me, but when 5 yards from me, he again suddenly fell, and landed this time on his breast with a sounding whack on the stones by the side of the loch. After a few seconds' pause to recover breath, he wriggled into the water and, when it was deep enough, dived. There were no eggs to be seen, and I do not know whether it was the male or the female who was guilty of this extraordinary performance.

Yrs., W.A.P.

1920

RECORD MAHSEER

SIR, WHILE FISHING ON THE Cauvery last Christmas, I had pleasure in witnessing the capture of the largest mahseer ever caught in India on rod and line. On being hooked by Colonel J.S. Rivett Carnac, it put up a tremendous fight, running out about 125 yards of line in her first great rush (so characteristic of the mahseer), and, had she kept on straight, a break was inevit-able, barely 5 yards of line remaining in the reel, but fortunately for the fisherman she turned and made upstream and the Colonel was able to recover line. After this the fish made several other big rushes, but there was line to spare. I was keeping time, and it was 25 minutes before we caught a glimpse of her, and when she was gaffed by Mr Bowring and drawn ashore, the excitement

The record manseer of 119 1b.

was so great that I quite forgot the timing. This mighty fish had the following measurements: weight 119 lb., length 64 in., girth 42 in. This old hen fish had a huge hog back and her body was almost cylindrical in shape. She must have seen many monsoon floods, and, judging from the age of the sacred fish in Mysore, she must have been quite 200 years old.

Yrs., EUGENE M. VAN INGEN, Mysore

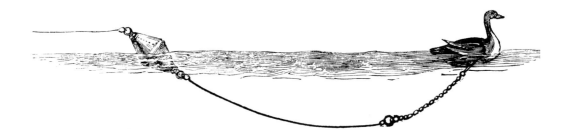

1922

SIGNS OF THE TIMES

SIR, A SIGN OF THE IMPROVING times as regards manly sports in place of dancing and poodle faking is the large number of officers, old and young, shooting in Kashmir this year. The number indeed is a record, and it is considered probable that it will be necessary to take steps to limit the number of men shooting, possibly by raising the fees for a licence. This is more likely to affect the married officer than the bachelor; the former is now going through a terrible time of high prices.

It is widely believed in India that the very poor show put up by Oxford this year in athletics etc., is due to the large amount of 'poodle faking' that is said to be rampant there. A number of men with sons about to leave school would be glad to hear if there is any truth in this widely-spread rumour. The inter 'Varsity ping-pong match has been the subject of much discussion out here.

Yrs., SPEAR

THE PSYCHOLOGY OF THE RABBIT

SIR, AMONG THE SUBJECTS for discussion by the British Association I noticed the other day was 'The Inadequacy of the Darwinian Theory,' and having twice in the week been witness to the tragic drama of a stoat and a rabbit, I could not but ponder how, under any system of the 'survival of the fittest', such things could be. In the one case, the rabbit, a familiar figure feeding on the lawn, had just retired to the shrubbery about breakfast time, when he returned, hopping right up to the house, and then describing a circle to the middle of the lawn, where he screamed and lay down, allowing a stoat, which had been following at some distance, to come up and seize him in the usual way. A gunshot ended their several careers. But here was this rabbit within a few yards of dense cover on the one side, or of open country on the other – either offering the readiest possible means of escape, which he would have joyfully used at the sight of a dog – simply putting up the white flag at first sight of his foe. In the other case, drawn by the scream, the gun arrived before the stoat had made actual contact; but even the shot and death of the stoat failed to galvanise the rabbit into activity, and it allowed itself to be caught by hand. How is it that with the immense mortality caused to the race in this way, a stouter moral fibre is not evolved? And why should the stoat and weasel – almost alone as far as I know amongst the beasts of prey – have his hunting made thus ridiculously easy? Has his evolution in the art of mesmerism outstripped for the moment the rabbit's defence – the ball, as it were, beaten the bat? Or is it merely a 'provision of Nature' for keeping in check the otherwise prolific little rodent?

Yrs., J.K.M.H.

ADVICE ON SHOOTING

SIR, I NOTICE A QUERY ASKING for information as to the authorship of the well-known lines of advice on shooting which end:

All the pheasants ever bred
Won't repay for one man dead.

My father, the late Mark Beaufoy, wrote these few verses for my benefit when I first began to shoot about the year 1900. If every lad was compelled to read, mark, learn, and inwardly digest these few lines of sound advice before being allowed to carry a gun, dangerous shots would become extinct.

Yrs., HENRY M. BEAUFOY,
Cowley, Oxford

[In response to requests from correspondents we print the verses asked for below in full – Ed.]

If a sportsman true you'd be,
Listen carefully to me:

Never, never let your gun
Pointed be at anyone:
That it may unloaded be
Matters not the least to me.

When a hedge or fence you cross
Though of time it cause a loss,
From the gun your cartridge take
For the greater safety's sake.

If 'twixt you and neighbouring gun
Birds may fly and beasts may run,
Let this maxim e'er be thine:
'Follow not across the line.'

Stops and beaters oft unseen
Lurk behind some leafy screen;
Calm and steady always be,
Never shoot where you can't see.

Keep your place and silent be
Game can hear and game can see:
Don't be greedy, better spared
Is a pheasant than one shared.

You may kill or you may miss,
But at all times think of this:
All the pheasants ever bred
Won't repay for one man dead!

So, if ever one flies low,
Prithee, sportsman, let him go.

BUTTERWORTH.HEATH.

1923

THE LATE LORD RIPON

SIR, AS ONE OF THE EXECUTORS of his will, I have before me the late Lord Ripon's personal game book, and it may be of interest to your readers to see the figures for the last few days of his life.

Sept.	Grouse.	Partridges.	Snipe.	Hares.	Rabbits.	Various.	Total
1...	–	110	1	11	–	–	122
3...	–	115	–	25	1	1	142
19...	194	–	1	–	–	–	195
21...	–	131	–	15	4	–	150
22...	158	–	1	–	–	–	159

On 22 September, Lord Ripon, at the last drive before his death, killed 51 grouse, and as the last birds were being brought in dropped dead in the heather.

The snipe, curious to relate, he missed with two shots, but, changing his gun with his usual rapidity, brought it down with his third shot.

Yrs., ELROWCLIFFE,
Hall Place, Cranleigh, Surrey

SPARROW HAWK ENTERING A HOUSE

SIR, TWO OR THREE DAYS AGO I was sitting in the drawing room with the windows open, and was startled by a small bird flying in pursued by a sparrow hawk. The small bird flew round and round the room so fast and making such a curious noise of terror I could not be sure what it was. It was closely followed by the hawk till it suddenly flew out of the window, and the hawk in trying to follow it crashed against the wooden sash of the window, breaking its neck and falling dead in the room. Is this not rather a curious thing to have happened?

Yrs., NANCY LUBBOCK

[Gratification of a compelling natural instinct, like the chase of prey, often leads birds and beasts into situations they carefully avoid at other times. – Ed.]

Shooting woodpigeons as they fly to the decoys

1924

USE FOR OLD TENNIS BALLS

SIR, MAY I MAKE MY ANNUAL appeal for old tennis balls to your readers who have so generously responded in previous years. The children in East and South-east London have received an enormous amount of delight from them, and I wish the senders could see for themselves what a joy a discarded tennis ball can still afford. Old cricket bats, childrens' toys, books and clothing are all most welcome if addressed to me here.

W.C. JOHNSON,
Toynbee Hall, 28 Commercial St,
London E1

FLESH-EATING CATTLE

Sir, Is not the eating of carrion by cattle unusual? A few days ago, in Ladakh, I noticed a young cow worrying something on the ground. I was some way off, and when I reached the spot I discovered it to be a dead chough. The cow had been busy shaking the bird to get rid of the feathers when I was first attracted by its action, and had eaten some meat off the breast – at least, I could not find any meat amongst the feathers she had scattered about, and the breasts were quite freshly eaten.

Yrs., C.E. DAVIES (Lt-Col.),
Sirmagar, Kashmir

[It is certainly unusual for cattle to eat meat, and the case recorded must be regarded as an instance of aberration of appetite. We believe, however, that in some of the remoter parts of Scotland, cattle are given smoked or salted fish in the winter when their natural food is scarce; and there is a case on record of an African antelope, a duiker, catching and eating mice. – Ed.]

Sir, No one who has fished in some of the remoter parts of the west of Ireland, or the Outer Hebrides, will be surprised at cattle eating anything. On a river I know in Co. Kerry the favourite food of the local cattle seems to be the hoods and upholstery of motor cars, rugs, luncheon hampers, or anything else that may be left unprotected. In the Island of Lewis boots are much favoured, also waders and landing-nets. And in both countries the local cattle have a perfect passion for the tops of fishing rods, and seem to prefer the best split cane. They would, no doubt, eat grouse too, if they could get them.

Yrs., B.

Sir, It may be of interest to mention that in 1895 the owner of a large station south of Sydney, N.S.W., told me he had just lost three of his best horses (yearlings) through eating the carcases of poisoned rabbits.

Yrs., H.G. PHILPOTT
(Capt., R.A.)

MYSTERIOUS KILLING OF SHEEP

Sir, I wonder if any of your readers can throw any light upon the following.

For some months past lamb-killing, and latterly sheep-killing, has been going on on the moors near here. The slaughter has been confined to an area about 2 miles long by 1 mile wide, bordering on cultivated farms.

Lambs have not been killed regularly or on consecutive nights, but intermittently, at times varying from 1 week to 3 weeks.

There are no marks about the legs, throats, or any part of the killed sheep, excepting that on each one a big hole has been made in the flank or groin in front of the hind leg; a big piece of the skin at this point has been torn off, but no wool has been removed or scattered about and no part has been eaten. Almost all of the dead animals have been found lying in a natural position as if asleep.

A few days ago a young shepherd saw the sheep, about half a mile off, running as if being chased, but he could not see anything chasing them. He ran to the flock as quickly as possible, and in doing so lost sight of the flock for a minute or two; he arrived at the spot just in time to see a lamb rising from the heather wounded as above, and as if some creature had just loosed it, but no creature was visible. This took place at 9 a.m., but most of the killing has been by night.

A careful watch has been kept by the shepherds on farms for miles around and no dogs have been found away from home at nights. Sheep killed by dogs are usually more or less mauled, and the above description makes it very difficult to believe that dogs are the malefactors.

I shall be very grateful if any of your readers can suggest a solution.

Yrs., T.A. WYNNE-EDWARDS
(Col.), Plas Nantglyn, Denbigh

Sir, Re. the mysterious killing of sheep, I should be inclined to put it down to the work of a pine-marten. Not so very many years ago in Lakeland pine-martens were as plentiful as foxes are now, and they killed both sheep and lambs, more particularly the latter. The wound in the flank or behind the shoulder corresponds to the place where a pine-marten would take hold. I believe there are still some pine-martens in Wales and the borders, and pole-cats are still quite plentiful there.

With the increase in foxes in Lakeland the pine-martens have decreased, although we still have some left, and one or two reach the taxidermists every year. Martens are great travellers, but if one has taken to sheep killing it would likely stay where such food was plentiful. Both terriers and hounds will run the line of a marten quite keenly and it should not be difficult to hunt the animal after picking up the line at daybreak near the scene of a killing. If the marten was put to ground, or marked underground, the smoke of burning bracken or grass would bolt it directly if the terriers could not do so. Martens are also not difficult to trap.

Yrs., RICHARD CLAPHAM

Sir, This weird but authentic story will interest those of your readers who are following the correspondence anent the 'mysterious killing of sheep':

Date about 1850. My grandfather farmed (as I do today) the home farm on his estate. His shepherd was one Simon Kinver. Sheep were being killed here and all around, their throats torn out as if by a dog. Kinver, armed with a gun, watched by night and by day, neighbouring farmers with their men doing the same. Dogs were shot on suspicion when unable to prove an *alibi*. Kinver shot several, and a man whose grandfather had a valued sheepdog has told me Kinver came to shoot it, declaring he had seen it worrying sheep. The owner held the dog in front of him and told Simon if he shot the dog he must shoot his owner too. Matters went from bad to worse. Kinver, apparently in despair at being unable to stop the slaughter, accused his fellow watchers of slackness with consequent troubles all round. At last suspicions were aroused. The shepherd was watched, more sheep were killed and footprints on marshy ground led to the sleeping Kinver, gun at his side, in a gorse brake where he had concealed himself to 'watch'. He was apprehended by Mr Adams, a tenant on this estate (and father of the famous Astronomer Royal, the discoverer of the planet Neptune), who, as 'parish constable', slipped handcuffs on Simon's hands after wisely discharging Simon's gun. He was transported and never heard of again. To add to the irony of the situation, my grandfather was chairman of the Cornwall Quarter Sessions, which fact evidently failed to impress his shepherd. The only reason I ever heard for this mad conduct was that a young lad was promoted as gamekeeper – a post to which Simon aspired. Kinver's method was to seize a sheep, tear out its windpipe with hands alone, fire his gun at an imaginary dog and then raise the alarm.

> Yrs., E.G. BARON
> LETHBRIDGE,
> Tregeare, Elgoskerry,
> N. Cornwall

1926

HABITS OF THE STOAT

SIR, THE FOLLOWING EXPERIENCE with a stoat which occurred to me last spring seems sufficiently unusual to place on record. When first seen it was carrying a very small young rabbit, of about the size at which they usually make their first appearance above ground. On sighting me it disappeared down a rabbit hole, taking its quarry with it. As this was close to the house, I got a gun and waited for it. After an interval of ten minutes or so the stoat suddenly popped out of the hole and made a dash across the open for the nearest covert, this time carrying in its mouth a round white object which I took, as I fired, to be an egg. As the stoat rolled over this white object fell from its mouth, and on picking it up I found it had all the appearance of being a small white cream cheese, about the size of a pigeon's egg. It was, in fact, the entire contents of the young rabbit's stomach – the milk which had formed the unfortunate baby's last meal in process of digestion. The stoat was a female just about to give birth to a litter of eleven young. In some districts in South Africa baboons have acquired the habit of killing lambs to obtain milk from their stomachs, but I have never come across a similar record in the case of a stoat. We know so little of the habits of small mammals in a wild state that this may not have been an exceptional instance. Had I not shot the stoat, I should have been left with the impression that I had seen it carrying an egg.

Yrs., A.L. BUTLER

1930

HATH MUSIC CHARMS

SIR, THERE HAS ALWAYS BEEN some doubt as to whether the howling of a dog when hearing music denotes pleasure or pain. Judging by the mournful sounds produced, one would be justified in assuming that he

A song with accompaniment

hates it, and is indicating as forcefully as possible his desire for the musicians to move on into the next alley. The case of the young performer in the photograph goes a long way to prove the contrary. For when less than a year old he started to play on his own initiative. Being somewhat diffident he would never do so when any-one was around, and for some days every-one was mystified when they heard the piano sounding, for upon entering the room nothing was to be seen but a small fox terrier gazing innocently out of the window. Very soon he began to sing to his own accompaniment, and so the truth was out. The performances have now become so frequent that the piano has to be closed part of the day, especially in the early morning. He usually strikes three notes, sometimes in the treble and sometimes in the bass, and then lifts up his voice in weird and wonderful song.

If he is not there and anyone strikes a note, he immediately dashes into the room and sits down expectantly, head on one side, plainly asking for more.

Yrs., C.M. CLARK,
Windermere

BIG SHOTS

Sir, We were six guns, and included in the team were, to use a cricket phrase, three 'England Players', Lord de Grey, Lord Ashburton and Prince Victor Duleep Singh. De Grey, as a shot, stood alone, the other two certainly in the first six. Duleep Singh was put on the right of a covert which was perched on top of a hill with a steep slope at the foot of which stood two of the guns, who were in the direct line of flight to another covert. Duleep Singh's legitimate rights were any pheasants breaking out right and any ground game there might be. A hen pheasant led the evacuation. Setting, from our point of view, an excellent example to her companions, she skimmed the wood and, seeing the forward guns, was about to rise and pass, a veritable little Gabriel, over one of them, when 'bang' went Duleep at about 30 ft., and that was her finish. More followed suit. So did Duleep. Then three more, six down and nothing for us. Such rotten pheasants for him, too! Damn the fellow!

Ashburton turned his back on it, and de Grey, in his high pitched voice, called out, 'Singh, Singh' in a remonstrating key. We gathered afterwards that Duleep didn't like being called 'Singh' and that really set him off. He had three guns and two loaders and kept going like a machine gun, and he shot 81 pheasants at almost point-blank range, and left us to deal with the remainder, which, as they all broke at his corner, were comparatively few. All the same, there was

Prince Victor Duleep Singh

astonishing merit in his performance. Incredible though it may appear, no less than 75 out of the 81 were perfectly fit for market. I say without hesitation that no man, living or dead, could have accomplished such a feat. There were no runners. Many of the birds were minus their heads.

Yrs., Lt-Col. CYRIL FOLEY

SPEEDY BEES

A GERMAN FARMER BET THAT 12 of his bees released 3 miles from their hive would arrive home at the same time as a similar number of pigeons liberated under the same conditions. The bees were powdered for identification; the first to enter its hive was a quarter of a minute in advance of the first pigeon, then three more bees arrived, and after that the second bird.

FLYING FLIES

SIR, WHEN FISHING ON Loch Leven one day last year, I experienced a curious phenomenon which may interest some of your readers. I was using a 10½ ft. rod, 4X gut cast and four flies tied on 000 hooks. It was a very sultry day with thunderclouds working backwards and forwards amongst the surrounding hills (no rain); consequently fishing was practically hopeless and I had to make the most of the sporadic 'catspaw' breezes.

It was about midday – and I had just made a cast more in faith than in hope – when the tail fly slowly rose from the water perpendicularly into the air and was followed by the other three flies. As they got higher into the air, they assumed a somewhat spiral movement, until the whole 10 ft. cast and four flies were serpenting in front of me about 12 ft. above the water. They were in the air approximately 3 minutes and then returned to the water rather more quickly than they had risen.

My wife and two boatmen were interested spectators, and one of the latter said that he had on a previous occasion seen one, the tail fly, rise a short way from the water, or should I rather say drawn from the water – the explanation being I believe, that the electricity in the air was acting as a magnet on the flies.

> Yrs., ALAN WHYTE-
> MELVILLE,
> Leith Fort, Edinburgh

UNLUCKY CARDHOLDER

SIR, I JOINED THE Political Department in 1897 as assistant to a Colonel J. at a small station where in normal times there were only two British officers. As plague had just broken out Government sent an IMS subultern and an Indian Army officer to assist in plague operations. In the evenings we used to play whist, and I noticed that Colonel J. held very bad cards, and scarcely ever won a rubber.

After a fortnight's regular play, I commented on this, and he told us that he had given up whist 20 years before as he always held such bad cards and that he only played with us so that we could get a rubber. His appalling luck continued for the next 2 months, when I had to leave for a tour in the district.

If there is such a thing as the law of averages, it may work in many ways. There may be the vast body of men who hold average cards, and the few abnormally lucky and unlucky cardholders. It is the same in all matters of life. Most of us have average luck, but we all know the fortunate person for whom everything seems to go right as well as the unlucky individual whose life is just one damn thing after another.

Yrs., E. O'BRIEN (Lt-Col.),
Woodlands, Kotagiri

Miss Alice DIPLARAKOU
Elected as Miss Greece of 1930, and subsequently chosen as Miss Europe, is fond of Currant Cake, for she believes that it is one of the few foods good for the health, and at the same time really nice to eat.

1931

FAMOUS CHARGER

SIR, I AM ANXIOUS TO KNOW if there are many officers' chargers which have the same record as a mare I own that is alive today. This, shortly, is her record. I joined the 2nd Life Guards in 1910, and in January 1911, I bought a black mare as a charger from Messrs Drage. She was foaled in 1904, and I purchased her in 1911 as a seven-year-old. I then rode her on all parades, which included escorts, guards, and guards-of-honour at Buckingham Palace. In August, 1914 I was out with the Expeditionary Force with the Household Cavalry Composite regiment, and took this mare with me, by name Suzette. I rode her all through the retreat from Mons, nearly to Paris, then the Battle of the Marne, up to Aisne, the First and Second battles of Ypres, Festubert, First and Second battles of the Somme; she continued to carry on the rest of the war and was ridden in the March retreat in 1918. The Household Cavalry were then dismounted and became a Machine-gun Battalion. I handed the mare over to the Brigadier-General commanding an Infantry Brigade, and he rode her through the final advance, and she ended the war at Mons, on the day of the Armistice, 1918, having completed the whole 4 years of the Great War. I got her back to England and hunted her for one season. I then started breeding from her and have bred five foals. Her first three carried the Holderness Hunt servants, including myself as Master. Her last foal was born recently, and is by the Lighthouse, and the mare's age is 27.

I should be most interested whether you know of any other mare with this record?

Yrs., ADRIAN BETHELL
(Capt.), Rise Park, Hull

[We should say that the career of this mare is quite exceptional, although Lt-Col. Geoffrey Brooke's charger Combined Training had a more or less similar record. – Ed.]

MULE

SIR, IN DECEMBER LAST TO celebrate the 150th anniversary of the rising of the Q.V.O. Madras Sappers and Miners, a reunion of their pensioners was held by the HQ of the Corps at Bangalore, South India. At every event of these celebrations prominent among the 2,000 pensioners was an ancient grey mule. This old veteran had joined the corps in 1891, presumably at the age of 5 or more, so now, in peaceful retirement, he must be at least 45 years old. His first campaign was Chitral, 1895. He afterwards saw service in Tirah, Malakand, 1897, Tibet, 1903, and the Abor Survey of 1911. In the Great War he accompanied the Indian Contingent to Egypt, and earned the battle honours of Egypt 1914–1917, and Palestine 1917–1918, being present at the defence of the Suez canal and the battles of Gaza and Sharon.

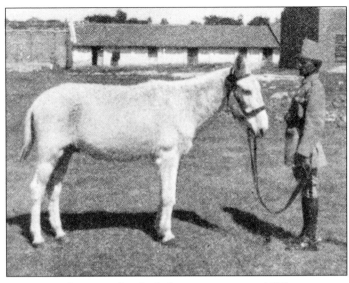

A grey mule which first saw service in 1895

His active career ended in 1922, since when he has roamed at large in the lines of the field troop at Bangalore. Though his teeth are few and very loose, he is generally to be found chewing happily in the vicinity of the feed room or forage barns. He is still very interested in life, visits most troop parades and, on occasions, has fits of great energy, when he will pursue an exercise party or ride for a considerable distance, even chucking a buck and a kick which many a two-year-old might well envy. He rarely strays far from the lines for long.

The same driver who led him at the Manakand was again on parade with him at the Pensioners' reunion last year.

Yrs., THE COMMANDANT,
Q.V.O. Madras etc., Bangalore,
S. India

COLOURS IN HORSES

SIR, A PROPOS OF THE correspondence on this subject, I do not know if the following rhyme has been quoted. It is the one I have always heard in Surrey.

One white leg, sell him if you can.
Two white legs, keep him for your man.
Three white legs, keep him for your
   wife.
Four white legs, ride him for your life.

I had a mare with three white legs, which carried me hunting for 9 years without a fall.

Yrs., E.D.B.,
Surrey

Sir, The following rhyme is current in Ireland:

One white foot buy him;
Two, try him,

Three, deny him.
Four white feet, and one white nose,
Cut off his head, and throw him to the
*   crows.*

In India horses of the last colour are considered the luckiest of all, and the most suitable for possession, and in that country without respect of age, shape, or soundness command a good price.

Yrs., A. BOXWELL, (Lt-Col.),
Gorey, Co. Wexford

1933

NEW WORDS

Sir, Megaphone being already in use, I suggest with good classical support 'macrophone' as a better word than 'loudspeaker'; also 'telephany' as more elegant than the clumsy hybrid 'television'.

Yrs., ARTHUR B. BROWNE (Rev), Bridlington

SPORT, GAMES AND PASTIMES

Sir, What a funny thing is language! Today the wrong use of words seems increasingly common. Anybody who picks up a daily paper will find in the index 'Sport, pp 6–10,' or something like that. If he were very young he might take the advice to back Bumble Puppy each way in the 3.30. But this, with the usual exceptions, will be as near as any information or news about sport as anybody can get that way.

So much has been written about sport that here it is intended only to differentiate between sport and other affairs. Sport, plain, without an article, is as different from 'a sport' or 'sports' as is chalk from cheese. To take an absurd instance, killing rats in a barn with a ferret and a terrier is sport; while polo between Jaipur and Osmaston, however sporting the play may be, is a game. Again riding a drag may be jolly good fun, but no argument can alter the fact that it is no nearer being sport than is trap shooting.

A list of those pursuits truly called sport is not very long, and as this letter is intended for the young, it may be a good plan to name them, more or less at random.

Hog hunting or pig-sticking, big game shooting, fishing, hunting with hounds (or cheetah), hawking, and small game shooting – these and these alone are Sport with a capital 'S'.

Sport in one sentence is the fair pursuit of some quarry, animal, bird or fish. There is a corollary, danger. This may be only the risk of being drowned in a salmon pool or peppered by a fool with a gun, but it is always there.

Now we come to racing. The danger is there; but racing is a 'sport', not 'Sport'. Mr Jorrocks called fox-hunting, not racing, 'the Sport of Kings, the image of war without its guilt and only 5 and 20 per cent of the danger.'

Boxing is or should be a sport. Then

Henley Regatta

there are many athletic tests of which the kernel is competition. Games have been dealt with so exhaustively that all we need say here is that for it to be said of a man that his game is sporting is the finest compliment.

Last, but not least, come pastimes, amongst which without seeming invidious, mountaineering may be placed first.

Yrs., J.A.H.
London SW

FIGHTING STAGS

SIR, ONE OF MY STALKERS, R.T. Cameron, was out at the end of the season to get venison for the house. He found nothing shootable on the top of the beat, and came down to the edge of the wood (scrub, oak and birch) where he had heard a stag roar. He saw presently a small stag with a hind within some 30 yards of him. Cameron saw the stag might improve and was watching him, when a big stag came out of the wood beyond like a bullet. The small stag ran some 10 yards towards Cameron before the big stag caught him, struck him with his antlers, chiefly in the neck and head (knocking out an eye, breaking a point off his horns and inflicting severe wounds in the neck).

The small stag was knocked down; his opponent backed 7 or 8 yards and then with lowered head struck him again and tossed him 5 or 6 ft. in the air. He then – he was probably not much more than 20 yards from Cameron – saw him and made off.

This small stag was terribly wounded but still alive, and Cameron put an end to its sufferings with a bullet in the neck. It weighed when brought home 10 st. 4 lb.

The victor in the unequal fight was a big stag. Cameron counted three points at one top, the other was so covered with hair and 'tallow' that he was unable to see it properly.

Yrs., J.N.W. NOBLE,
Ardkinglas, Argyll

TAPING TIGERS

SIR, A SHORT WHILE AGO A veteran tiger-shot, now retired in Kenya, informed me that tigers shot by people of eminence were often measured with special tapes – metal or cloth – on which an inch measured about 9/10ths of an inch only. Hence a 10 ft. tiger would measure at least 11 ft. This would, I fancy, deceive any unwary A.D.C. or similar individual deputed to measure the big man's victim.

Yrs., 'ARME BLANCHE',
Risalpur

SURPRISED BLACKBIRD

SIR, NOT LONG AGO I was near my goldfish pond in the garden when I heard a splashing and looked round to see a hen blackbird having a bath in the bird bath at one corner of the pond above the deep water. She had her tail hanging over the edge of the bird bath and just touching the surface of the pond. As I turned, my big golden orfe – 12 in. long and named Old Bill – spotted the feathers on the surface, made a swift dash from the depths, and seizing them, gave a great tug. The moment he tasted feathers he let go and swung off disgustedly.

At the same moment the blackbird, who had been pulled into a squatting posture by the old fish's mighty tug, was looking round in a puzzled manner to see who was playing tricks with her tail, and after shaking the water from her wings flew off.

Old Bill is a veritable glutton; he sticks at nothing, and has eaten my four newts.

Yrs., A.F. MORDAUNT SMITH, Richmond, Surrey

CURIOUS MARKINGS ON WINDOW PANE

SIR, ONE DAY TO OUR astonishment the picture of a large bird appeared on a large plate-glass window of the billiard room of my house. There had been a bright moonlight night and it seemed to have been an owl which had left its ghost-like impression on the glass. From the enclosed photograph the curious impression is quite visible.

I think the owl had been flying on a moonlight night against the reflection of the window. There is a similar window on the other side of the room, and it might even have looked right through the two.

Yrs., C.F.G.R. SCHWERDT, Old Arlesford House, Arlesford, Hants

The ghost-like impression of an owl

1934

TOP HATS FOR HUNTING

SIR, WHAT SHOCKINGLY UGLY hats the modern silk toppers are! Low and a little bell-topped. Why not the real sporting shape, 'the neck or nothing'? That is a slightly truncated cone in shape with the point upwards. The old Duke of Wellington is seen wearing this pattern in one of the several pictures in which he appears out hunting. Quite a chapter might be written on top hats. The early ones would not stand a wet day, as the silk was fixed to the frame by glue, and the wet soon caused the silk to slide off. It was not till the shellac frame was invented that a topper would go through a season. The very ugliest form was the immense chimney-pot of the '50s and '60s. It was King Edward, when Prince of Wales, who reduced the 12–13 in. hats to a more moderate height of about 8 in. When I lived in town I had a block made to fit me. The pattern so produced I always wore and found that I was 'in the fashion' about every four or five years. The present fashion is more like a pile of muffins on a plate than a hat.

Yrs., TOPPER,
Kent

The Prince of Wales on his
way to the meet

VETERAN BRIDGE PLAYER

Sir, The enclosed photograph may interest *Field* readers. It shows Mrs Grieg, the widow of the famous composer playing bridge at an hotel in Norway. She plays bridge with three others until 11 p.m. every night, and the ages of the four players add up to 363. Her age is 82.

Yrs., D.G. WRAITH,
41 Branksome Wood Rd,
Bournemouth

Widow of a famous composer

INDIAN SUPERSTITION

Sir, From Southern India to Kashmir, wherever bears are found, the jungle tribes firmly believe that male bears abduct native women and after keeping them for a while, let them go.

Are there any grounds for this belief?

It is understandable that a jungle family with this bar sinister in its pedigree should keep the matter quiet, but surely their neighbours would talk.

I have frequently made enquiries into the matter but could never find anything definite or any known case to support it.

Yrs., F.W.A. PRIDEAUX

Sir, In answer to your correspondent on Indian superstitions, I met with the same belief in bears abducting native women, at just the opposite end of Asia, in the Verkhoyansk district of Takutia. I was supplied with the name of a woman thus abducted three or four years previously (I was there in April 1905). I tried to ascertain the facts; they were quite plain. A young woman went into the forest and did not return. Her husband searched in vain. After about 2 months, in the autumn, she returned and related to her husband and to all who cared to listen, that she was captured by a big brown bear, placed in a den and fed on hares, willow-grouse, berries, etc., but in the autumn the bear became sleepy and she managed to escape.

The husband was glad to recover his missing wife, and seemed to believe all that she said (as husbands often do). As to myself, as I was a Justice of the Peace during more than 20 years (before the Revolution), I have my own ideas on the sort of evidence such tales of missing wives to their husbands constitute.

Yrs., S.A. BUTURLIN,
FMBOU, Moscow, USSR

1935

TIGER CLIMBING TREE

Sir, A FRIEND AND I were shooting over Easter in the Mandala division in the C.P., and had both wounded the same tigress in a beat. She lay up some 200 yards behind our 'machans' and was quite visible to one of our 'longstops,' two of whom had been posted about 150 yards behind us. As she was not visible from any other position it was decided that I should climb the tree which was a 'Sal' which had no branches for the first 25 ft. and about 12 in. in diameter, taking with me a cord with which to draw up my rifle. Having climbed to about 20 ft. I became exhausted, and called to the man 5 ft. above me to come down and help me up the remaining distance. When this man commenced to climb down the tigress charged. My friend and our 'shikari' who were standing within a few yards of the tree both fired, which made her pull up at the base of the tree. She then looked up at me and proceeded to shin up the tree like a domestic cat without effort, and seized me by the right leg. After my friend's third shot she fell, tearing a number of muscles out of my leg. Her topmost claw marks were measured the next day, and taped exactly 18 ft. I have spoken to a number of people with big game experience varying from 20 to 40 years and have only heard of one instance when a tiger climbed a tree with the lowest branch some 12 feet from the ground to *avoid* danger. I suspect my case was sheer bad luck.

Yrs., M.A. FOOKS,
British Military Hospital,
Jubbulpore, C.P.

DEAD DONKEYS

Sir, I WONDER HOW MANY OF your readers have seen a dead donkey. At a dinner party the other night the question was raised and I was the only person who had seen one.

I remember it quite well, it was about ten years before the war, when I was travelling down to Newmarket for the races. Looking out of the window I saw one on its back in a field as dead as a door nail.

I cried out, 'There's a dead donkey,' and was nearly torn to pieces as everybody in the carriage wanted to see it.

I believe it is considered lucky. Anyway, myself and a friend had a very good day, and I so seldom get one it must be true.

Yrs., HAROLD BALE,
Stoneydeep House, Teddington

[129]

1936

EGG-STEALING STOAT

SIR, YOUR CORRESPONDENT IS SURELY wrong in supposing that egg-stealing by stoats is *rare*. Although they may have to roll hen's eggs, they can deal much better with partridges. My keeper saw a stoat carrying an egg. He shot the stoat and brought me the egg undamaged except for the small holes at the small end of the egg where its teeth had just punctured the shell in order to obtain a grip. He said it looked as if the stoat was running along balancing the egg on the end of its nose!

Yrs., DOUGLAS
CARRUTHERS,
Barmers Hall, King's Lynn

SAFETY FOR AIR USERS

SIR, IT SEEMS INCREDIBLE – perhaps not a little humorous – that a flier can, in these days, actually fail to find not only a village, but even a city in this small country of England, yet this has often been our experience.

There are many days when clouds lie low on the hills, and visibility is reduced to about 100 yds. How are pilots to find their way with only a few square yards of ground visibility to guide them and no sign-posts to tell them where they are?

The only answer is to fly dangerously low over a railway station, until the name on the platform can be read. It is useless to tell us of the risk. We know it, but we are up in the air and must come down. We naturally want to do this either at our destination or at some aerodrome. Otherwise, the alternative is forced landing.

The safety of the flying man or woman, and that of their passengers, would be helped enormously by the simple use of a few pots of paint for display of signs on the roofs of gasometers or other outstanding buildings.

We would be the last to suggest that the country should be splashed far and wide with garish signs for the convenience of flying people, but there could be little objection to those painted on the roofs of flat buildings as they would be visible only from the air.

Yet whose is the responsibility for safeguarding the interests of those in the air? If a village has a notorious 'Death Trap' on its road it surely feels its liability? In the same way, do not cities and towns hemmed in by smoke-ridden skies make the air dangerous for pilots who are trying to find their way through visibility which is almost nil?

Local authorities, whether with or without aerodromes in their vicinity, usually feel they have no responsibility in the matter, yet a simple name sign-posting a town or village would not only be of inestimable value to aviators and help to ensure public safety in the air, but would prove also to be a tremendous municipal advertisement.

Yrs., AMY MOLLISON
J.A. MOLLISON,
The Gatehouse, London SW

HOOPOE IN SCOTLAND

SIR, ON 14 SEPTEMBER AT Alt-Na-Bea, five deer-stalkers and I watched for some time through our glasses at a distance of about 60 or 70 yds. a bird which has since been identified as a hoopoe. It seems to have been feeding on flies or grit. It was soon joined by five or six sparrows, and a starling, who all seemed as surprised at its appearance as we were.

My wife, who is President of the Royal Society for the Protection of Birds, hopes very much indeed that it may not be killed.

Yrs., PORTLAND,
Berriedale, Caithness

1937

THE LITTLE SHIKARI

SIR, I ENCLOSE THE PHOTOGRAPH which, I think, may be of interest to your readers. The boy's father, Raja Maharatendra Singh, of Pauna, gave me the photograph. The boy shot the cub, entirely unaided with a .22 saloon rifle firing a long cartridge – one shot only. It was a male tiger cub, measuring 6 ft. 3 in. The boy's age is 6 years 4 months.

Yrs., P.V. HARRIS (Lt-Col.),
17/21 Lancers, Meerut, U.P.

'There was a little man and he had a little gun'

TENT CLUB CASUALTIES

SIR, LAST YEAR, IN AN ACCOUNT of the Nairo Moro Tent Club, I mentioned that the bag had suffered from heavy casualties to horses and spears. The Chairman of the Club has had several bad smashes, resulting in bones going. The Hon. Secretary was picked up unconscious a short time ago, and the writer has been unable to ride for a year as the result of a smash while riding pig; and now Captain Eric Gooch, one of the founders of the club, has been killed by a fall while riding a pig. The going is, perhaps, too easy, and the pace consequently too fast, for in 30 years in India, no such casualties occurred. It rather looks as though the age limit for hog hunting is under 50 years of age. Captain Eric Gooch was a great sportsman; he owned one of the biggest and most successful racing stables in Kenya, and not only had an exceptionally good eye for a horse but was a very clever horse master. He was much handicapped while riding pig as he had a stiff leg, unfortunately on the spear side. The Nairo Moro Tent Club can now muster only two spears.

Yrs., 'SPEAR', KIKIYEE,
Kenya

A STALKER'S SHOT

SIR, WHILE I WAS OUT stalking with Mr Whyte-Melville-Skeffington on the home beat on 29 September he shot a stag stone dead through the back of the head going full gallop, stern on, at 740 yds. Mr Skeffington would never have taken such a risky shot but for the fact that it was a fine old 11-pointer with a great span of 30½ in.

He had been trying to get in to this stag all day, but was prevented owing to the great number of hinds.

At last, late in the evening, in a very bad light he decided to try a shot at him at about 600 yds. which he did when a good broadside chance offered. The bullet went about 6 in. over the stag's back. He immediately went off at a full gallop but got the second bullet in the back of the head as he slowed back for a moment against some white scree. The stag came down head over heels like a bolting rabbit. I have seen Mr Skeffington do many a good long galloping shot, but never one like that. I believe he has shot over 1,000 red deer, stags and hinds, out of which he has only wounded six! He always does his own stalking and never uses telescopic sights. He tried telescopic sights on a .22 rabbit rifle once, but never hit a thing. I thought I had better write to you about this long shot, which I think must be very nearly a record.

Yrs., COLIN MACPHAIL,
Knock House, Isle of Mull

Sir, I was surprised to read a communication from a stalker in the Isle of Mull who apparently sees fit (1) to encourage his gentlemen to take a running shot at a good stag in bad light at an impossible range. (2) claims credit for having established a most unpleasant kind of long-distance record. (3) has the audacity to state 'I have seen many a long galloping shot but never one like that' – a shot fired apparently by the same sportsman who had killed over 1,000 deer to his own rifle and only wounded six!

I would ask Colin Macphail whether he has at heart the interests of deer forests or deer stalking when he broadcasts to the sporting world a 740 yds. fluke through the medium of your newspaper. I for one would prefer to forget about it.

Yrs., LOVAT,
H.M. Tower of London EC3

Sir, There is, however, one side to the question which strikes me as remarkable. Mr Skeffington – I find on reference to *Debrett* – is aged 22. Say he began stalking at the tender age of 14, he had shot – according to his Boswell – his 1,000 red deer in eight years, or more than 100 a year. The same book of reference tells me that his home forest is an island one, and it must indeed be prolific, as it is quite obvious – if the stalker is in the habit of shooting at 700 yds. – that most of his stalking is done at home.

Yrs., 'DEERSTALKER',
Inverness

A morning leap: a hind jumps a 6ft. 6in. wire fence early on a misty day on
Exmoor

FALL OF TREES

SIR, A SOMEWHAT REMARKABLE incident occurred here one Saturday recently.

About 2 p.m. on that day a group of beech trees, six in number, standing on a slight slope in a meadow, suddenly opened out like a fan and fell – one to the north, one to the south, two to the east, and two to the west.

There was no wind, and the trees were in full leaf, and were about 80 to 90 years old.

They all ripped up the surrounding ground, leaving great chasms from 4 ft. to 6 ft. deep. The ground was hard and dry. I think the explanation of this may be that the trees were originally planted too close, and the lateral branches were only on the outer side.

Possibly the dry weather had something to do with the simultaneous fall of these trees. The curious part of the matter is that the trees should have all fallen at the same time. The ground at the roots was hard and stony, and the roots were very dry, and in some cases rotten, but the foliage looked quite healthy.

Yrs., C.P. CRANE,
Warleigh Manor, Bath

FEEDING A SEA-GULL

SIR, I WAS RETURNING FROM Guernsey by steamer a few weeks ago, when, rather bored with the crossing and a few sandwich crusts, I amused myself throwing bits of bread to the gulls in flight. One bird in particular became a faithful crust eater. So I attempted to feed him by hand, but was forced to employ gradual steps – throwing the bread less far each time. Eventually the gull became fully confident that I was no fraud and snatched from my hand every offering I could afford.

Obsessed with the idea for a stroll I left Albert – as I christened the gull – to roam the seas. Upon returning, I observed a young man, standing exactly where I had stood some 5 minutes previously, trying his utmost to entice a gull to carry off some bread from his hand. The gull seemed frightened and paid no attention. I watched this until the young man gave up his project and retired to his cabin. I then produced my last sandwich and offered it to the gull. He swooped down and calmly flew away with more than a beakful. I repeated this several times and concluded that I had met Albert the Faithful again.

This proved that not only could Albert discover that I was the genuine article, but he also learnt to recognise me and shun imitations.

Yrs., VINCENT NORRIS,
Sandhurst

DEALING WITH MOLES

SIR, YOUR READERS MIGHT BE interested to know that it is a common belief here that moles may be driven away by pouring urine into their runs. I have done this during the past two years and I believe in its efficacy.

Yrs., FRANK A. STOKES,
Johannesburg

FOOT AND MOUTH DISEASE

SIR, I HAVE FOR MANY YEARS past watched the seasonal incidence of foot and mouth disease, and coupled with it the arrival of the foreign onion sellers whom one sees about the country on foot or on bicycle.

So certain have I been of the fact that these men and their onions are spreaders of the disease that when motoring through the country with my wife one or other of us on meeting an onion seller always makes a remark that we shall soon hear of an outbreak – and we seldom fail to hear of one.

It would be interesting to know how many of these men have been wandering about Norfolk, Suffolk, Kent and Sussex lately – all coastal counties with harbours, where these fellows could land their strings of onions.

Yrs., E.W. BROOKS,
Nettlebed House, Oxon

1939

FLEAS ON THE DECREASE

SIR, IT OCCURS TO ME THAT A change has taken place as regards to these. Some years ago it was a common or usual experience to pick up a flea, if one travelled by train or 'bus or visited a theatre.

For years now I have not seen a flea, though my habits have been the same; and one or two solutions appear probable; perhaps you can decide which is correct. Either there are fewer fleas about or, alternatively, they only go for younger people. (I am no longer young.)

Yrs., GEORGE DICKINSON,
Warwick and County Club

Sir, It is probable that human fleas are generally much fewer in numbers owing to the widespread use of the vacuum cleaner. This machine is infinitely more effective than a brush in removing dust etc., from mats and carpets, the places where the flea lays her eggs. The now very popular custom of smoking in trains, buses and theatres may also have something to do with their decrease in numbers. As a non-smoker I have often noticed the strong smell of tobacco smoke when taking off my jacket in my room, after an evening at the cinema. This may serve as a repellent. However I must admit I have occasionally picked up a flea in some public vehicle or place of entertainment.

As regards a host; doubtless the flea prefers to pierce the skin and imbibe the blood of a child rather than resort to a not-so-easy middle-aged, or elderly person. Forty-five years ago, when I was 12, an attack was made on me in bed at a boarding house in Brighton by several fleas, but in a night or two a liberal sprinkling of pyrethrum powder had got rid of the invaders.

Yrs., CAMERON SHORE,
15 Bristol Road, Brighton 7

RIGHT AND LEFT

Sir, While walking with Mr George Adamson, Assistant Game Warden, along the bank of the Uasso Nyiro River one night, a guinea fowl got up and was shot by the Warden.

The sound of the shot caused an 8 ft. long crocodile to leave a recess beneath some rocks and rush towards the river. The Game Warden killed it with his remaining barrel, and completed a remarkable right and left.

Yrs., 'SPEAR',
Isiolo, Kenya Colony

1940

SPARROW HAWK AND LARK

SIR, RECENTLY, WHEN FISHING on Loch Griam in Sutherlandshire, the boatman and I had a curious experience. While rowing along the shore of the lake, twenty yards out, a sparrow hawk came round the hillside and stooped at a lark. A dozen times he got above it and dived down on it from 100 feet, but every time when he had nearly succeeded the lark, seeing it could not reach the shelter of the heather, shot up above him, so that the hawk had to circle up once more to get overhead. At last the lark obviously began to tire, when suddenly, instead of shooting up into the air above the hawk, it flew out to our boat and settled on the end of my rod, which was lying across the boat. The hawk swooped down on it at terrific speed, but I threw my cap in the air and yelled just before he reached the lark, and he swerved up into the air and flew off across the lake. The tiny lark, panting with exhaustion, sat at the top end of the rod gazing out anxiously, its body trembling with fear, until the hawk was out of sight, and then it turned round and looked at me and moved sideways right up to the rod, almost to my hand, and, after keeping its eyes fixed on me for at least a minute, gave two cheeps and flew off to the heather on the shore.

The boatman and I sat dumbfounded. He was a crofter. Then he said 'That is the most wonderful thing I have ever seen in nature.'

Yrs., GEORGE CHARLTON,
Woodford Lodge, Kettering

AMMUNITION FOR PARASHOTS

SIR, I HAVE READ WITH interest the letters in *The Field* on the subject of suitable cartridges in shot-guns, for use against parachutists. I may be wrong, but it is difficult to convince me that there is not considerable danger in using, especially in old guns whose barrels are thin, any shot cartridge almost cut through above the powder charge.

Up to a few years ago, there was on the market, a cartridge loaded with 'Rodda' patent Rotax bullet. This could be had for 12, 16 and 20-bore choke or cylinder guns, and was most effective against tiger, leopard, pig or crocodile. It was most accurate, and had great penetration: the muzzle velocity was in the region of

1,200 ft., per second, and the muzzle energy about 1,700 ft. pounds.

Another point. According to the Geneva Convention, the bore of cartridges for use in civilised warfare was laid down: not exceeding .303 for the rifle, although the service revolver was .45. What will be the position of anyone taken by enemy forces and found using any of the cartridges recommended for 12-bore guns, and which are expanding and above .303?

The third point is, can parachutists be shot before the 12th?

Yrs., J.C.C. FOOTT,
Helmsley, York

[The practice of firing a cut cartridge is dangerous as it increases barrel pressure. A safer plan of this sort is to fire that portion from a 16-bore cartridge which contains the shot-load from a 12-bore cartridge whose shot has been removed. Even then a fully choked barrel might be bulged.

We quite agree with all you say about the Rotax bullet. It gives good results from the ordinary game gun and has great smashing power against medium game. Until the beginning of the present war it was certainly procurable. But it is a hollow-pointed bullet. The use of a shotgun in civilised warfare is legal, we understand, so long as hollow bullets are not employed.

There is no close season for parachutists. – Ed.]

1943

SHOOTING HARES

Sir, When I was at school at Amesbury, the head, the Rev. E. Meyrick, who was a well-known archer, used to shoot hares with a bow and arrow. I believe the Plain then belonged to Sir Edmund Antrobus. It is wonderful what a paralysing effect an arrow has. Years ago I and my brother, through reading *Gustave Almardo Indian Tales*, had a scouting battle with bows and arrows and he put one through my leg. I could not move, and the withdrawal was very painful.

Yrs., W.H. HEATH,
Upton Dean, Andover, Hants

THE ELUSIVE CORNCRAKE

Sir, My experience suggests that the number of corncrakes varies inversely with the mileage of telegraph and telephone wires. Corncrake on toast is not unknown here. The texture of the meat is as of pheasant, the taste as of guinea fowl.

Considering that in the teeth of competition for freshly killed or crippled birds, from buzzards, ravens, carrion crows, herring gulls, blackbacks, rats and whatnot, the islanders find some, one cannot but wonder what is the total toll taken by some of the few wires on this 1,000 acres.

The bird likes to sing from an eminence – a molehill will serve. One craked regularly from the sawn-off stump of a shrub about 15 in. high within 10 ft. of my window. I knew of several nests 20 miles south of London two decades ago, but people in that district began to 'Say it by telephone' and the birds disappeared.

Ornithologists noting an occurrence of corncrakes might do a service if they remarked upon the presence or absence of wires in the vicinity.

Yrs., MARTIN COLES
HARMON, Lundy,
Bristol Channel

THE HOMING INSTINCT

SIR, THE FOLLOWING INCIDENT seems to me to be phenomenal and worthy of record.

My unit had three pigeons, two of a local variety similar to the 'Homer'. The pigeons were for some time in one camp, then moved several miles to another where they lived in a crate.

When the advance of the 8th Army started the pigeons were moved many miles into the desert where the unit stopped for several days, so the pigeons were allowed their liberty and used to fly around the camp and perch on either one of the piles of stores or on the vehicles.

The unit received sudden orders to move and the pigeons could not be caught, so the birds were left behind, the unit moving on 80 miles by train and the unit vehicles following by road the next day, 13 November.

From the point of detrainment the company moved on by road transport together with its own vehicles which had rejoined the company, and eventually encamped another 70 miles on in the desert, surrounded by many other units and much debris left by the enemy.

The company was travelling for two days, and its vehicles for one day, arriving in this location in the evening of 15 November. On the morning of 16 November the pigeons rejoined the unit, having pursued it for approximately 150 miles over desert and where there was a constant stream of troops and vehicles moving.

The pigeons may have followed the company transport or may have been flying around and from the air recognised five white leghorns which are carried around also with the company.

I appreciate that 'Homers' are trained to fly back to their cotes and homes from considerable distances, but it seems to me quite phenomenal that they should pursue their cotes when they are moved away 150 miles and dumped amidst a seething mass of troops and vehicles, and when the tentage and vehicles of all are much the same pattern.

Yrs., LESLIE A. OMEROD,
(Major)

1944

A COLOURLESS RAINBOW

Sir, It was 6 p.m. on the evening of 5 July, the sky was a ceiling of low cloud, there was no sign of rain. A flying bomb passed overhead out of sight, I stopped, waited, and looked. The bomb fell out of the cloud a mile away in open country. As it hit the ground a 'shimmer' of the shape and width of a rainbow appeared – a complete half hoop centred on the bomb. It was there and it was gone, seconds passed before smoke was seen to rise and the sound of the 'crash' was heard. The top half of the hoop was 10 or perhaps 15 degrees above the horizon.

The appearance of the bow was completely positive and completely sudden, that is to say it did not fade away or alter so long as it was there; and it was there for an instant.

Yrs., W.R. PARNALL,
Junior United Service Club

WAR AG DIRECTIVE

Sir, Can any of your readers help me with advice on how to carry out the following order issued by the 'Pest' Department of the War Agricultural Committee?

'Within 28 days all rabbits to be destroyed and each hole to be filled with stones and earth or other suitable material'.

The land in question is about 800 acres of woodland.

Yrs., 'IGNORANT'

[We can only suggest that the Pest Officer is pushed into one of the holes. – Ed.]

ENJOYABLE

Sir, Round about the year 1894, when cramming for Sandhurst, in London I often used to go to a certain well-known grill-room in Piccadilly and get there a lunch which I still remember. It was served *A la carte*, and centred round a mutton chop of a size and lusciousness I never see now, and it worked out thus:

Loin chop, 10d.; fried potatoes, 1d.; vegetable, 1d.; roll of white bread, 1d.; pat of butter, 1d.; chunk of cheese, 1d.; glass of beer, 2d.; waiter, 1d.; total 1/6.

A dash of Worcester or Harvey sauce was as free as the salt.

Nor was this all, for the other ingredients of a pleasant meal were all there. There was no crowd, no delay. You went straight into a big clean room with no tobacco smoke polluting the air, plenty of room between the tables and plenty of elbow room at them, and you spent the time waiting for what you had ordered in watching a chef in a long white coat cooking it on an electro-plated grid over a clear charcoal fire. You then had it deftly served by a waiter at once who knew his job to the end.

You went away really satisfied and could, on your way home, get an ounce of Navy-cut tobacco for 4 ½d. and a first-class pipe to smoke it in for five bob. You might find the tax-collector waiting for you on your return but you could make him quite happy by giving him 5d. in the pound.

On my return to England at the close of the 1914–1918 war I thought I would do it again, but it was not to be. I found the same building with the same name but everything else had altered for the worse beyond recognition. In an over-crowded room, foul with tobacco smoke and noise, I got a badly cooked mass-produced meal slapped at me for 5/-, without the beer. I have not tried again and will not, but I left the place sorrowing and muttering, as I sign myself now.

Yrs., 'ICHABOD NOSTALGIA'

STRANGE BEHAVIOUR OF A DOG

SIR, SIX YEARS AGO I found a stray greyhound lying beside the road about 200 yards from my avenue gate. He was in a bad state, starving, and the pads of his feet worn bare and bleeding. I carried him home, fed and nursed him back to health.

No owner ever turned up for him, so he continued to live here. Of late he had been gradually failing, and one night he was missing, and in the morning was found dead, lying in *exactly* the same place where I found him six years ago. It seemed very queer to me how he went away to die in the very same place where he had lain down to die all that time before.

Yrs., BETTY McCHEANE,
Wellbrook, Freshford,
Co. Kilkenny, S. Ireland

EFFECTS OF DDT

SIR, IT IS ANNOUNCED THAT DDT is shortly to be put on the market as an insecticide. It will certainly be used in large quantities by farmers and gardeners, for its effectiveness is almost legendary. I hope we shall watch that our friends the birds do not suffer as a result of this chemical, not because DDT is lethal to them – I believe this is not so – but because it may destroy their food.

Further, if you kill the cabbage whites you presumably also destroy the red admirals, the commas and the tortoiseshells, while the prospect of DDT among the fly life of a chalk stream is too horrible to contemplate.

We have interfered with the balance of nature before with unfortunate consequences. It is only with full knowledge of the dangers that we should launch such an atomic bomb as DDT on the insect world.

Yrs., MICHAEL C. PLATTEN,
6 Wetherford Close, Wesley
Park, Birmingham 29

WHEEL STOPS

SIR, WHILE WALKING UP THE hill at Windsor recently I noticed pieces of iron let into the kerb and the gutter and could not imagine what the purpose could be. I was still wondering as I continued on my way, when the mystery was solved. A horse-drawn cab had its back wheel resting on the iron thus being prevented from running backwards down the hill.

I have never seen anything of this nature anywhere else in England but feel that it must be a custom dating back a great many years. No doubt with the re-appearance of the horse on the roads during the war years the wheel stops have again been put to a useful purpose.

Yrs., J.A. FISHLOCK,
3 Coopers Lane, Grove Park
SE12

USE FOR FLAMETHROWERS

SIR, I HAVE NOT SO FAR been able to see the petroleum warfare exhibition in London, but it has occurred to me that if some of the more obsolete types of flamethrowers are being disposed of by the War Office, they might prove to be a help in solving some of our problems on the land. A tracked vehicle with two of the larger types should be able to act as a deterrent to bracken if applied at the right time of year and should cover a far larger acreage per diem than any of the existing cutters. It would penetrate into rocky corries and boulder-strewn ground where no vehicle could go. It may prove to be the answer to this pest which has spread so much in recent years.

Again, flamethrowers should be a big help in clearing the vast areas where wood has been cut during the war and the debris is still unburnt. I would also suggest that the pack type be tried on nettles and thistles, and as a weed killer generally.

Probably someone with knowledge of their effect could say whether, if judiciously applied, hedges could be scorched with them to an extent which would check the growth without radically damaging the hedge. If this could be done the weeds which grow along the bank at the foot of the hedge could be killed or checked at the same time.

If such information can now be divulged it would be interesting to hear some statistics as to range and fuel consumption and the working costs, both of a suitable carrier and of the actual flamethrower.

Another use to which I suggest it might be put is to scorch patches of sphagnum moss with a view to killing the ticks which in my humble opinion are largely responsible for the present general shortage of grouse.

A.G.C. COLQUHOUN,
Littleton Farm, Shepperton

1950

SHOOTING PARTY, 1899

SIR, I AM SENDING YOU A photograph of a shooting party in 1899, which I think will interest many of your readers. The authenticity of this extraordinary picture is vouched for by Mr Jim Lawson, who keeps the Crown here and in whose bar parlour I first saw it hanging.

I believe the sportsmen portrayed came from neighbouring towns, and brought their own beaters with them. This was presumably because the men at Martley held that discretion was the better part of valour. The beaters in the picture seem happy enough, however, in spite of the fact that the lad on the right has a gun pointing straight at his chest, and the one sitting down looks as if he might have his head blown off.

The gentleman with the pipe, nonchalantly leaning against the tree, is quite

Careless rapture

happy because, you see, his hammers are not back!

The masher on the left with the whiskers is pointing his gun straight across a right of way. I would not care to walk partridges next to him on the smoothest ground – indeed under no circumstances would I have shot in the company of any of them. If only one of them had his gun over his shoulder with the triggers down, this would have been the perfect illustration of how not to hold a gun.

The paucity of the bag suggests that, if dangerous to themselves, they were not equally dangerous to the fur and feather they sought.

It is interesting, however, to record that I believe all died a natural death, though probably with a good few pellets under the skin.

Yrs., G. HOWARD HEATON,
Martley, nr. Worcester

RACING AT BULAWAYO

SIR, THE ACCOMPANYING photograph is a photofinish of the Stayer's Handicap 'C' Division (One Mile) run at a meeting of the Bulawayo Turf Club, Southern Rhodesia, on 18 March 1950.

Chaprak, ridden by T. Stuart (nearest

A close finish

camera) won by a short head, and Claro, ridden by A. Macklin (centre) beat Trapper, ridden by apprentice E.T. Halfpenny, by the same distance.

The Bulawayo Turf Club races under the Rules of the Jockey Club of South Africa and Meetings are held on 24 days a year.

Yrs., J.H. CROSSLEY,
Bulawayo

AN AGGRESSIVE OWL

SIR, THE FOLLOWING ACCOUNT OF an owl defending its young may prove of some interest to readers.

One exceptionally sunny morning last May, I was walking through a wood when I noticed a young owl perched in a low cleft of a lime tree, and only about 18 in. from the ground. It was still covered with grey down, and its eyes were blue like a young kitten's. Thinking that it had fallen from its nest, and fearing that a weasel would destroy it, I bent over the owlet intending to lift it to a higher bough. As I stooped I received quite a powerful blow on the head and something tore at my scalp.

On recovering my balance I found the back of my head covered with blood. The youngster remained totally unruffled, but on looking up I was just in time to see the hen bird coming in to attack again while the male watched from another tree. I cannot but think I was very fortunate to have been looking down and not up when the bird attacked.

Yrs., D. COHAM-FLEMING,
Coham, Black Torrington,
Beaworthy, Devon

AQUATIC RABBIT

SIR, WHILE WALKING ALONG the Tweed at Coldstream recently, I was surprised to see a young rabbit make its way over the pebbles and enter the water. It swam out about 3 yards, then returned to the bank where it remained for some time, half in and half out of the water. It then proceeded to swim in a small circle and return to the bank to be chased ashore by an inquisitive jackdaw. I have seen rabbits enter the water when chased by dogs, but have never heard of a rabbit swimming for pleasure. Three people witnessed the occurrence and there was no doubt that it was a rabbit, and not a water vole.

Yrs., R.A. LAINPREY,
Grenofen, Alnwick

EXPERIMENT WITH CHIVE

SIR, READERS MAY LIKE TO know of an experiment which was made to ascertain how many and which kind of insects visit one individual chive plant in the course of 12 hours.

The main visitors were bees, the first one making its appearance at 6.50 a.m. Each bee, as it alighted on the plant, received a dab with a paint brush, and thus it was found that, with few exceptions, the same bees came again and again to the chive, while comparatively few other insects visited the plant. The last bee came about 7 p.m.

Altogether, 12 bees made 71 visits to the chive, while the other visitors were one June-beetle, one fly and 12 gnats, making a total of 85 visits.

Yrs., E.O. HOPE,
Horsmondon, Kent

VAGARIES OF FLIGHT

SIR, ONE FINE MORNING in the distant past found me seated comfortably on the ground, somewhere in front of the club house at St Anne's. I was waiting for the finish of a game, in which a friend of mine was taking part, and the lunch which was in prospect. When the players at last came within reach (I am not a golfer) of the final hole, I called to my friend to know if I was likely to be in their way where I was sitting. 'No,' he shouted, 'not at all, and you are quite safe too.' I must have been at least 20 yards from him, on his right. He made his stroke and sliced the ball which hit me a crack on the head I did not forget for a week. Indeed a vagary of flight! In spite of it I was able to enjoy an excellent, though profusely apologetic, lunch.

Yrs., J. RAINE,
Bramblewood, Fawkham, Kent

UNREQUITED LOVE

SIR, THERE IS A long narrow loch in Scotland at one end of which lived two swans, a male and a female; at the other end of which lived two geese, also a male and a female. Neither pair was ever known to cross an imaginary centre line.

In the hard winter of '47 the female swan was frozen into the loch and died, and the male swan immediately joined up with the geese. The female goose took this as a personal triumph and for the next year flirted outrageously with the swan, who paid not the slightest attention. The male goose, in the meantime, became more and more dejected.

At last the swan could stand it no longer and paddled back to his original beat, the female goose following in great excitement, puffing and blowing. But the swan took her by the neck, drowned her and threw her into the rushes.

Now the whole scene is changed, the male birds will not let each other out of their sight and paddle round chuckling all day, the greatest of friends.

Yrs., J. EDWIN FORBES,
London W1

DO SWALLOWS TAKE DRAGONFLIES?

SIR, I HAVE LIVED ALL MY life in districts where swallows and dragonflies were plentiful, but I cannot recall an incident in which a swallow was seen to attack a dragonfly.

There is a particularly lovely, rather small, blue dragonfly, which, on one Kintyre loch, is excessively numerous in the month of August, when the insects lay their eggs. You can watch the skimming sand-martins for an hour, and never see one of those tiny birds tackle a dragonfly. Besides the small, blue dragonfly, Kintyre has at least three other varieties of dragonfly. There is a giant variety which is rather rare, and I have had a pair of these come at me like angry bees more than once. Then there is a rather large, and a rather small 'heather' dragonfly, and not once have I seen a swallow of any variety tackle one.

As a boy, I tried out my trained merlins at the giant dragonflies, but although those clever little hawks readily tackle birds they were certainly afraid to tackle a dragonfly.

It would be interesting to hear what other readers of *The Field* have to say on the subject of dragonfly immunity from swallow attack. I have not observed that kestrels take dragonflies, but observations of the castings of those birds should disclose whether the dragonfly is a frequent victim of the kestrel.

Yrs., DUGALD MACINTYRE,
St Agathe, Oban

CAN ANIMALS SEE PICTURES?

SIR, THERE IS IN OUR HOUSE at Porlock a half-length picture of a lady, a relative of mine, long since dead. The portrait expresses her vivid personality and the eyes seem to follow you all round the room.

Some ten years ago a visitor called, bringing with him a pointer dog. When I entered the room I noticed that the dog was trembling and obviously frightened. Thinking I might be the cause of its alarm, I spoke to it; it was quite friendly, but still went on trembling. I then realised that the dog was gazing fixedly at the picture. His master dragged the animal, vehemently protesting, to the portrait, and made him smell it. After that the dog became quiescent.

A few months ago a lady brought a poodle to our house, and the same thing happened. The dog whined and barked and showed signs of fear, but was reassured after smelling at the portrait. I have recently been told of a cat which always spat at a picture of a cat whenever it passed the portrait.

Yrs., E.W. HENDY,
Holt Anstiss, Porlock

Sir, I have a golden retriever and during the last war we had been out shooting and decided to have lunch in the local inn. Whilst having our lunch in the bar parlour, the others of the party drew my attention to my retriever who had got up on to a seat, above which hung a picture advertising a noted brewery's beer, and beside the beer on a plate was a loaf of bread and a large chunk of cheese. My dog was trying to grab the bread off the picture.

Incidentally, this dog has a passion for loaves of bread and steals one if he has a chance. It also speaks well for the artist being able to deceive my dog.

Yrs., L.E.F. BARNARD,
Oakly Park, Ludlow, Salop

BIRDS AND DECAYING TREES

SIR, MOST PEOPLE KNOW THAT elm trees can be very dangerous due to decay from the centre which does not show itself on the outside until the final cracking of the tree in a wind. For many years I have thought that birds know when a tree has begun to decay and is dangerous, and readers may be interested in the following observations.

Two large elm trees had nests in their tops for at least ten years. The birds ceased to build in them and five years later these trees made no fresh foliage and showed dead twigs at the top. Ten years later they were cut down and found to be rotten and dangerous. An elm which had plenty of foliage and nesting sites, never had birds' nests although the birds built in surrounding trees. This particular tree was blown down last month and found to be completely rotted through at the base.

Another elm has had no nests in it for about ten years although the birds did build in it before then. Last week I decided to examine this tree and cut the top portion.

It was rotten from the centre to within 3 in. of the bark and yet has thick foliage and shows no sign of decay from the outside.

I wonder if any reader has ever seen an elm, fallen from decay, which brought down with it a bird's nest. Perhaps the birds can recognise a 'smell of death' in trees.

Yrs., JOHN CLARK,
163 Allerton Rd, Liverpool 18

Sir, In reply to Mr John Clark, I can say that I have, but in most cases the nests were built in an adjoining tree, the boughs of which were intertwined with the boughs of the decayed tree; in the remaining cases the trees had fallen owing to recent unusually severe storms.

In my younger days, when I did a lot of bird watching, combined at times with forestry, I noticed that certain birds, particularly carrion crows, rooks and magpies, avoided a decayed tree when selecting a site for their nest. Furthermore, sound trees marked for felling, blazed and numbered, were also avoided by the birds. One year when marking was late, I saw a pair of magpies, having commenced to build a nest in such a tree before it was marked, cease building and chatter with anger at daybreak the day after it was marked, and commence to build a nest in a tree not so marked.

I have also seen a pair of old magpies come and inspect such a nest and then make a young pair, obviously building for the first time, give up and start again in an undamaged tree.

I noticed also that an old pair of birds always inspect a tree from all angles before they commenced a nest. They always started on the ground and worked up the trunk, then they tried the boughs outward, and then from the top inwards. If a fault were discovered, the mate was always summoned to look at it.

I have told these details to many people, but it was obvious that most of them did not believe me. My experience of birds has taught me that they have far more practical common sense than most people believe.

Yrs., 'THE GREY CHAPE'

THE FIRST SALMON

SIR, WHEN I CAUGHT MY first salmon in the last week of September, on the River Deveron, I can only describe it as one of the grandest and most thrilling moments of my life. To hook a salmon, the sudden check to the fly, the tightening of the line, the tug, and the scream of the reel – is there anything like it? As I am in my seventies, and this was my first attempt, I felt it a great triumph.

The fish gave five terrifying leaps before I managed to get level with him, and by climbing up the back I got him well in hand. But to my intense relief my husband turned up at the right moment, and gaffed a fine fish of 10½ lb.

Lady Legard with her 19-pounder

Our last day on the beat was a red letter day – between the hours of 4 and 6 p.m., in torrents of rain and an icy cold south-east wind, we hooked and landed five fish, and I had the great good luck to hook and kill a 19-pounder – a beautiful fresh, clean female fish. The fish took 17 hectic and exciting minutes to play from a slippery muddy bank and a difficult foothold.

We staggered home – a good mile, ending up a steep hill – laden with 61 lb. of fish and all our fishing gear, soaked to our very skins, but never happier.

> Yrs., E. LEGARD (Lady),
> Malton

1953

STARTING A ROOKERY

SIR, IN YOUR ISSUE OF 16 April the question of how to start a rookery is raised. My father achieved this nearly 70 years ago by placing some artificial nests (black coloured baskets of the appropriate shapes and sizes) at the top of several Spanish chestnut trees and filling them with train grease, at that time used for lubricating the wheels of railway carriages and trucks. This attracted the birds and before long they started to build their nests, not in the chestnuts, but in some tall adjacent poplars. In a few years a colony of 40 to 50 nests was established. It lasted until the trees were cut down a few years ago.

Yrs., E.H. TOMLINSON,
(Lt-Col.),
Atlow, nr. Ashbourne,
Derbyshire

Sir, My grandmother, noticing that rooks, probably from a rookery about a mile away, nearly always appeared when she threw household scraps on to the lawn for the smaller birds, asked her baker to deliver each day five loaves extra to the requirements of the house. These were chopped up into lumps of about a cubic inch and one of the under-gardeners was given the job of dumping a big basketful of bread on the lawn below the trees. In the second year that this was done three or four rooks started nesting. She carried on the custom for about ten years before her death, and she always had a small rookery of about a dozen nests. This I may add was some 40 to 45 years ago.

Yrs., C. HAMILTON SHAW
(Maj.),
South Gate, Avenue Road,
Wolverhampton

MORNING SONGSTER

SIR, AS I LIE IN BED I see a cherry tree outside my window against a dark background of pines. At about 5 o'clock each morning a blackbird perches in the cherry tree and sings. The other morning I was surprised to see its breath condensing to a little white cloud each time it sang – it looked almost as though it were smoking a cigarette. The same thing happened the next morning, which was also frosty.

Everyone has noticed a horse's breath on a cold day, but am I very unobservant to have reached the age of 60 before noticing the same thing when a bird sings?

Yrs., COLIN J. SMITHELLS,
Chalfont St Peter, Bucks.

1956

ELEPHANT DID NOT FORGET

SIR, EVERY SPRING 'Lord' George Sanger's circus used to pass our house. Once a young friend and myself were standing in our gateway when the elephant passed; one big fellow put his trunk over the gate towards us and my young companion, very naughtily, tickled it with a piece of holly. The elephant withdrew his trunk quickly and trumpeted loudly. The next spring as the circus passed our house one of the elephants seized our gate, pulled it off the hinges and threw it across the road – he had not forgotten.

Yrs., V.R. JARVIS,
Dorchester, Dorset

QUEEN'S PORTRAIT

SIR, IN THE PICTURE OF Her Majesty, it seems a pity that the artist should have depicted this well-known horse with the neck of a stallion, an unpulled tail, an untrimmed mane and with his forelock kind of 'shingled'.

Sir, Any of your readers who have not seen Sir Alfred Munnings' magnificent exhibitions of paintings at Burlington House will have missed a great treat. But it is a pity he continues to make his horses walk with the gait of camels – compare the horse and the pony in No. 106 – and all his hunt servants use double-bridles.

Yrs., E.J. BRIDGES, (Lt-Col.),
Cavalry Club, London W

Sir, For 60 years I have studied horses. I have kept many in the past and still possess a few, my last purchase being Bunker II, by Djebel, at Sandown Park last year. I have studied action always. I know every position of the walk by heart.

If Colonel Bridges will go down on all fours he will find himself walking exactly as a four-footed beast walks. Starting with the off-hind foot going down first; simultaneously the off-fore goes forward and is next on the ground. Next comes the rear-hind, then the near fore. I have watched the scene in the paddock before each race for years and I have watched the action of the horses on the far side, led by the lads in succession, until the jockeys get up and off they go. These scenes have given me untold pleasure. Let any reader, at the next

The Queen's latest portrait, painted by Edward
Seago. The Queen is wearing the uniform of
Colonel-in-Chief of the Coldstream Guards which
she wore at the Birthday Parade. She is riding the
police horse, Winston. The picture will be hung in
the Officers' Mess of the Coldstream Guards at
Wellington Barracks.

meeting he or she attends, watch the led horses. Let him try shutting the eyes and instantaneously opening and shutting them for a while and all the various actions are seen.

My favourite position of horses at a walk is with a forefoot going down, as in 'A Royal Ascot postillion and bay horses at Windsor Castle Mews'. This position makes the best design.

With reference to the pictures of hunt servants (only a few are shown), riding with double bridles. I have merely painted them with their horses bridled as they were when they stood or sat for me. To instance two portraits, one of Freeman on Pilot, the other of Barker, the present huntsman of the Pytchley, both men had their horses bridled as I painted them. I always used a double bridle when I used to give myself a day out with hounds.

Yrs., ALFRED MUNNINGS,
Dedham, Colchester

GUN LICENCE GAME

SIR, WHILE THE GUNS AT a Boxing Day shoot were walking along a road to the next beat, they met a police constable on a bicycle. The constable demanded to see the guns' licences, whereupon one of the guns, a short fat little man, nipped through a hedge and ran across a field. The constable dropped his bicycle and gave chase, catch- ing up with the fugitive some three fields away. After fumbling in his pocket, the fat man duly produced his licence. He was the only one in the party who possessed one!

Yrs., D.H.R. GIFFORD
(Lt-Col.), Wimborne Road,
Bournemouth

FLYING TRAY

SIR, JUST BEFORE GETTING up time one morning I heard fluttering sounds and was paralysed with astonishment on sitting up to see what was happening.

A small silver tray had apparently taken off from the dressing table and was cavorting round the room on vibrating wings, scattering its contents over the floor and bed. Leaning over at a perilous angle, I saw that the wings belonged to a bird – unmistakably a bird which seemed to be in violent combat with the silver tray.

After some frantic flutters and cheeps, the tray was left defeated upon the floor while the bird flew to a perch on the looking glass for a preening of feathers and outraged feelings. Then I recognised him as a blue tit with rakish eye and untidy plumage – an old friend.

The solution is, presumably, that he came on a friendly visit, settled on the edge of the tray and got his long curved claws entangled in the filigreed pattern. The tray is of Indian silver, very light in weight, so the tit was able to fly with his unwelcome burden for a few moments before collapsing.

Yrs., P.M. LYLE,
Sway, Hampshire

RED SQUIRREL MYSTERY

SIR, WITH THE ADVENT OF the grey squirrel and the disappearance of the red squirrel coinciding, it was, more or less, taken for granted that the reds and the greys could not live together, and one was inclined to presume, rightly or wrongly, that the greys were killing off the reds.

I have not, as yet, come across anybody who has seen any evidence of the massacre; no corpses, bones or tails strewn about, and it is hardly conceivable that a grey would kill a red without leaving some traces.

It would be interesting to know if any of your readers have had some experience which might throw some light on the mystery as to where the red squirrels have gone.

Yrs., R.S. MAXWELL,
Exmouth, Devon

Sir, In, or about 1922, when I was pathologist to the Zoological Society, I received the body of a red squirrel from a lady in Scotland. She stated that she had found several corpses and wanted to know the cause.

Our helminthologist found a small roundworm in the duodenum, which he identified as the cause of death. Unfortunately not being a helminthologist myself I have forgotten its name.

I may add that at the time the grey squirrel had not reached Scotland and I am not sure that it has now. It would look, therefore, rather as if an epidemic of this worm disease might well be the cause of the disappearance of the red squirrel.

Yrs., N.I. LUCAS,
East Grinstead

1957

DETERGENTS AND THE SKIN

SIR, THE GREATEST SKIN specialist since Phineas Abrahams died 40 years ago told me that a great number of his patients came to him with a superficial rash. In his opinion, this was entirely caused by one of these much-advertised detergents being used in the washing of their underclothes.

Many skins, he told me, were allergic to the ingredients. He named one in particular, but I do not wish to fight a libel action.

Yrs., H.J. BUCKMASTER,
Buck's Club, London W1

BALL LIGHTNING

SIR, MY PERSONAL EXPERIENCE happened in 1905, and I am now in my 87th year, but in vivid memory can still see the marvellous ball of fire. In the course of a heavy thunderstorm at Wargrave on Thames, Berks., in company with a professional fisherman, I saw an outstanding example of this uncommon occurrence.

We were perfectly sober and sane and had no doubt about the quality of our eyesight! We were in a punt endeavouring to get from a high bank on the South Oxfordshire side of the river some shelter from the heavy driving rain.

The ball descended to the opposite bank and apparently was about 2 to 2½ ft. in diameter; it ran slowly along the sedgy margin for about 60 yards then immediately in front of a pile of the camp shedding and a large willow butt, which it appeared to impact, exploded with a terrific rolling bang after which the atmosphere became delightfully fresh and carried an ozone chemical smell. The ball was flame coloured, but the explosion produced a mixture of colours. The width of the river is about 40 yards.

My companion, who unfortunately is no longer alive to confirm this story, was much shaken and frightened, but being of a very cool and placid nature, I 'took it in my stride'.

I have experienced some very severe storms round Africa, in South America and the West Indies and have not seen another example of ball lightning, but have seen exceptionally heavy rainfall at Mombasa and Zanzibar, one Christmas day storm at the latter produced 9¼ in. of rain.

Yrs., A. EDWARD HOBBS,
The Retreat, Woodstock, Oxon

Sir, Some 50 or more years ago I went to play in a croquet match at Haywards Heath. We played, I think, on the cricket field. There had been a drought and the ground was like iron. Presently a thunderstorm came on with torrential rain, and in a few moments the water was lying on the ground. We huddled into a small tent near the court. I was standing at the door looking out, when, accompanied by a deafening crash, an egg-shaped ball of fire fell a few yards from the tent. As it struck the ground the water splashed up with a loud hiss. In size and shape it resembled a pheasant's egg. People there at the time spoke of it as a thunderbolt.

> Yrs., M. PARSONS (Miss),
> Mousehole, Forest Row, Sussex

Sir, As a boy at a preparatory school – Dunchurch Hall, near Rugby – I experienced this phenomenon. It was in the summer of, I think, 1894, and there was a terrific thunderstorm, which began in the morning and went on till late evening. This apparition of a 'lightning ball' had been seen by various people in the neighbourhood hovering about for some time. In the evening, when we boys were all in bed, it took a dive over the house, and struck a large Wellingtonia in front of the house and blew it to pieces, leaving only a stump four to five feet high. No one was hurt and I do not remember that there was any damage to the house, but pieces of the tree were blown great distances down the field below.

I told my mother about it. She was then at a French spa and, in answering, told me she had mentioned the matter to a French scientist there, and he had confirmed that *lumière en balle* – as I recollect he called it – was a well-known, though rare, occurrence.

> Yrs., LAWRENCE EARLE,
> Eastbourne

Sir, In the early '90s we lived in a street paved with Mountsorrel granite blocks. During a heavy thunderstorm the rain was hitting the granites and bouncing back as a spray to a height of 5 or 6 inches. Down the street, bouncing on the spray, came a ball of fire the size of a youth's football. I watched it until it reached the stone-surfaced high road where it 'grounded', bursting with a terrific flash. No damage was done save that I could not see for several minutes, but the house and the street smelled strongly of sulphuretted hydrogen.

> Yrs., E.A.C. HUSBANDS,
> 16 Bridgegate, Retford, Notts.

CAPTURING A PURPLE EMPEROR

SIR, IMAGINE A SCENE ON a June day when it is 80 degrees in the shade: mother, father and four small boys are languidly exploring the wooded lanes of Holmwood Common, Surrey, hopefully carrying butterfly nets, when suddenly there is a shout from

Father: 'A white admiral' – and they all converge on the sunny glade, only to watch the beautiful creature disdainfully dipping and gliding high out of reach amongst the oak branches.

It avoided capture, and the family eventually arrived back at the Land Rover hot and dispirited. In bundled the children, thinking of cold, fizzing lemonade and cherries waiting to refresh them at home.

Suddenly there is a piercing shriek, 'Daddy, Daddy, a purple emperor,' and believe it or not, there, settled inside the Land Rover, quietly awaiting capture, was a purple emperor, one of Britain's most sought-after butterflies. It could not have been a more fitting end to a birthday outing – and if you do not believe it you may come and see the specimen for yourself.

Yrs., MARGARET CLARK,
North Holmwood, Surrey

CHIVALRY BY A STOAT

SIR, IT IS SELDOM ONE thinks of stoats as kindly creatures, but after witnessing the following rather unusual happening perhaps a few commendable words will not be amiss. A male and a female stoat were crossing the River Hebden in the Hardcastle Craggs area, and as the river was in flood the stoats were attempting to cross by jumping from rock to rock, the male leading the way.

Nearing the middle of the river, the female jumped short and slipped, but though most of the hind part of her body was swaying about in the rush of the flood she still managed to retain a hold on the smooth wet stone with her front paws. On noticing the predicament his mate was in, the male immediately turned back, and without the slightest hesitation quickly gripped hold of her by the scruff of the neck and forcefully dragged her out of the rushing torrent to safety. He released his hold when he had pulled her to the topmost part of the rock, then without further ado the pair continued their journey successfully to the opposite bank of the river.

Though stoats are noted for their callous ferocity, the witnessing of such a happening proves that even these killers can at times act kindly, at least with their own species.

Yrs., F. DEAN,
Mytholmroyd, Yorkshire

HORSES WITH SHEEP

SIR, WE BRED A CLYDESDALE filly who showed a very unpleasant temperament from her youngest days. When walking our dogs where this filly was grazing, she would leave her companions and deliberately go for the dogs, and not in a playful manner. When two years old, she killed a sheep, which performance she repeated a few weeks later, and was seen doing it.

We never put her with sheep again, but kept her; however she was never reliable and always had a peculiar temper.

> Yrs., EDITH HEDLEY,
> Grove Place, Nursling, Hants

Sir, My neighbour kept losing sheep and he put the killing down to dogs. The police and his own men had a special watch kept and he put up a tent for them to watch from. Our men were working in the next field and they saw one of my friend's Irish hunters in the act of killing a sheep. It picked up quite a big ewe by the neck with its mouth and was striking it with his forefeet. Our men called to the watchers. 'Here is your sheep-killer.' So the mystery was solved.

> Yrs., M. PRICE-OWEN,
> Brompton, Cross Houses,
> Shropshire

A MAN-TRAP WARNING

SIR, WITH REFERENCE TO the query about man-traps, I have one in my possession, which belonged to my great-grandfather. He has been described as being a man of ready wit and prompt action; when orchard robbing was prevalent and the perpetrators could not be traced, he obtained a human leg from a surgeon at a distance, had the amputated limb placed in a man-trap which had been found in his orchard, and directed the local crier to go his round and 'cry' the ghastly relic; no one claimed the leg, of course, but no one after that molested the orchard.

> Yrs., 'SHADOW',
> Stirtloe House, Buckden,
> Huntingdon

ANGLER HOOKS DRAGONFLY

SIR, THE FOLLOWING INCIDENT occurred recently while I was fishing on a friend's trout stream in the New Forest. I reeled in to the length of my eight-foot cast, on which was tied a small alder fly. As I was endeavouring to catch my fly in my left hand in order to secure it to my rod in preparation for walking back to the house, a gust of wind blew it away from me, and at that very moment, when the wind was keeping it more or less stationary in the air a few feet from me and on a level with my eyes, a fully grown yellow-striped dragonfly suddenly checked its flight within about 6 inches of it, then moved forward to seize it. As it did so I gave the rod a tiny jerk, and to my astonishment I had the insect hooked.

I played it for several flights as far as my cast and the extended rod could reach, but it quickly tired, and I could have caught it quite easily, but refrained from doing so as I did not wish to crush it. I let it escape, apparently none the worse for its ordeal.

My friends have suggested I should write to you to inquire whether any readers have had a similar experience.

Yrs., J.H. LANGMEAD,
Flansham House, Flansham,
Sussex

MR COX'S PIPPIN

SIR, MR CHARLES WORTH asks in *The Field* how the Cox's orange apples came by that name. On the Bath road at Cranford there is the Berkeley Hotel. Nearby is a lovely avenue of elms planted in Charles II's reign, leading to Cranford House, the home of the earls of Berkeley. On the London side of this avenue lived a gentleman named Cox, whose hobby was raising fruit trees, plants, etc. From a certain apple pip he grew a fruit tree and crossed it with an old Blenheim orange apple tree, which is noted for its keeping qualities, and so he called this new apple Cox's orange apple pippin.

Yrs., BERT NOY,
East Cornworthy, South Devon

Sir, Mr Noy is not quite correct. The apple was raised not by Mr Cox of Cranford, but by Mr Richard Cox, a retired Bermondsey brewer, at The Lawn Cottage, Colnbrook, Buckinghamshire, in 1830. Lawn Cottage still stands, apparently little changed. The tree, growing in the vegetable garden and visible from the house, was blown down in 1911. The seed parent was a Ribston Pippin and the pollen parent believed to be a Blenheim Orange. Out of nine seeds sown in a pot were produced Cox's Orange Pippin and Cox's Pomona. The history of Cox's Orange has been closely investigated and is recorded in A. Simmonds's fascinating *Horticultural Who Was Who* published in 1948, with cloth binding, and all for only 3s.

Yrs., G. ST CLAIR FIELDEN,
London W1

KITES AND TOBACCO

SIR, SOME YEARS AGO in India, I was taking a stroll with a friend enjoying my morning cheroot when a kite swooped down and snatched it out of my mouth. The theft was made so suddenly that I had no time to ward off the bird. All I felt was a slight touch of a wing on my face.

Yrs., C.F. READER,
London W1

WASPS' NESTS

SIR, I KNOW OF NOTHING more instantaneously lethal to wasps than petrol – sprayed from a syringe. Wasps on the wing can be 'shot down' with the petrol mist that the syringe will discharge.

Yrs., HUMPHREY SWANN,
Truro, Cornwall

HOW TO FIND WASPS' NESTS

SIR, WE HAVE HEARD A lot about methods of destroying wasps' nests, but the really difficult question is seldom mentioned – how to find the nests in the first place. Recently an elderly and much-travelled lady who came to tea with us told us how it should be done. You wait till the wasps are buzzing round the jam on the table and you capture one under a tumbler. Then take a piece of fine cotton to one end of which is tied a fragment of tissue paper. On the other end a loop is made, and raising the edge of the glass you lasso the wasp round the waist with this loop and draw it tight. Now comes the exciting part. Go outside, release the wasp, and keeping the tissue paper in view pursue it to its lair.

I asked this lady if she could do it, and she said she could; so I captured a wasp under a tumbler for her, and prepared the other items required, and waited expectantly. She got the tissue paper on and the loop ready, but when she raised the edge of the tumbler the wasp flew out. She apologised for her shaky hand and advancing years and asked for another wasp, which I provided. She cleaned her spectacles and made another attempt. This time she took much longer, but the same thing happened. Having provided her with a third wasp, I took a piece of cotton of my own and wandered into the next room where a number of wasps were crawling up the window. Rather to my surprise I managed to lasso one of these quite easily. I rushed outside making hunting noises, and when all were assembled, I released my wasp. But it flatly refused to take to the air and merely lay on its back kicking and stinging the cotton. I should have liked to take off the cotton, and let it go in acknowledgement of the thrill it had given me, but this would have been altogether too hazardous, and I was forced to kill it.

Later I happened to find the nest without scientific aids and it was interesting to view the wasp-line course which my elderly lady would have had to follow had she carried through her project. She would have gone through my wife's herbaceous border (then in full flower), over a thick laurel hedge, down a six-foot drop, over a boggy patch for 50 yards, and up to the top of a nearly vertical bank covered with brambles.

I was not at all certain whether I was having my leg pulled and I made some enquiries, the result of which leads me to believe that some such method is really practiced in Australia. But even there I should prefer, I think, to be mounted for the pursuit. I wonder if any of your readers have first-hand knowledge.

Yrs., E.E. NOTT-BOWER
(Brig.), Holyford Close,
Colyford, Devon

Sir, Many years ago, when a boy in Lincolnshire, I tried the method he describes of tying a piece of white cotton round a wasp's waist. But I did not use the tissue paper as a marker.

My experience was different from the Brigadier's. On each occasion the wasp flew to a mulberry tree on the lawn of my old home and proceeded to bite through the cotton.

Yrs., J.C. SALE,
Foxley, nr. Dereham, Norfolk

Sir, My 13-year-old son successfully found wasps' nests last summer by the following method.

He first attached a cotton with a little resin to a wasp held very gently with tweezers, but found that it invariably removed it. He then put the wasp in a very small vice he made and lassoed it with a slip knot in the cotton. After experimenting patiently for a long time he found that a wasp can become airborne with only a short length of cotton and that bright red is the best colour for the chase.

The first wasp was excitedly followed by the whole family to its nest, which was fortunately in a bank on the edge of the pond at no great distance.

The second wasp took off over the vegetable garden. Twice it alighted in the raspberry canes, and my son released it by picking up the end of the cotton. It then gained height, but came to grief again in an apple tree. He climbed the tree and hand launched it again, but this time as it gained height the wind caught it and it zoomed over the roof of the stable and out of sight.

Yrs., Mrs MARGARET J.
KEMBALL, Hurrell Farm,
Boxford, Essex

1958

THE NOT-SO-VEGETARIAN TROUT

SIR, RECENTLY ON THE Birdsgrove length of the Dove, a few trout rising were particularly fastidious and disposed to inspect critically an artificial fly before turning away to continue feeding.

The contents of the stomach of one of the more adventurous comprised the following: green aphis, large pale-green flies, four bluebottles, many willowflies, red ants, three small bees, two wasps, a few dark olives, many small black flies resembling diminutive house flies and a quantity of the seeds of agrimony.

And yet the fish were so discriminating!

Yrs., N.E.P. HARRIS,
The Red House, Trysull,
Wolverhampton

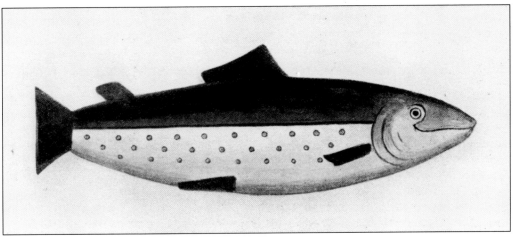

A trout of 1672

A TIGER'S JUMP

SIR, I ONCE STAYED AS A guest of the late Maharajah of Dholpur in his pink sand- stone Moghul guest house. He was unlike most Indian princes in that he had given up shooting and taken to watching and preserving the game in his State. He told me how once in his shooting days a young tigress in her prime of life was being driven up a nullah one side of which was a vertical wall of rock and so high that they had not troubled to put stops on that flank.

The tigress, finding that she was trapped, took one look at the rock wall and bounded up it. This so astonished the guns that they measured it and found it to be 32 feet. There was no question of a 'take off' half-way up. As a result the Maharajah had all his permanent machans raised considerably.

Being the man he was I entirely accepted this astonishing figure and I suppose if you consider the vertical height a domestic cat can jump it is not impossible. I should be most interested to hear of other readers' comments or experiences.

I would add that the Maharajah had himself trained a herd of sambur deer – I think he said it took him seven years. I went with him into the scrub jungle round his palace and he called up the herd and then put his arm round the big stag's neck – a truly remarkable performance.

Yrs., R.K. PAGE (Lt-Col.)
Grange Con, Co. Wicklow

A PIGEON'S CURIOUS DEATH

SIR, I HAVE RECEIVED A letter from my son, aged 15, who is at school in Cheshire, telling me of a curious incident. I quote from this letter: 'A very odd thing happened on Thursday afternoon. I was walking near the Peacock Drive when I saw a pigeon fly out of the bird sanctuary quite normally. I said to the boy who was with me: 'What a lovely shot!' and I went through the motions of firing a gun: the bird circled and then fell to the ground with blood coming from its head . . .' This, surely, was a most curious happening.

Yrs., ELIZABETH TAITT,
Belnagarrow, Craigellachie,
Banffshire

Sir, When I was in Walton Hospital, Liverpool, one of my few interests was to watch the semi-tame pigeons flying outside my one small window. One afternoon one of these birds, after circling outside, alighted on the top of the open sash window and promptly toppled over to fall dead within the room. I did not regard this as a particularly auspicious omen. When a nurse showed me the corpse I could not detect any sign of injury.

Yrs., COOMBE RICHARDS,
King's Caple, Herefordshire

Sir, In your 31 July issue there is a letter referring to a pigeon falling dead when a schoolboy went through the motions of firing a gun at it. I am afraid I should have found it hard to believe the incident if it were not that I had once had an almost similar experience.

At a covert shoot in Angus my stand was in the garden of the lodge. This was surrounded by high beech trees, and a cock pheasant came over above them, perhaps about 100 to 120 ft. up. I put up my gun to shoot it, but before I fired it swerved and fell dead and was picked up. There was no shot fired by any other gun. I had a companion standing beside me for a witness. There was no loader and we were shooting with only one gun.

This has remained a mystery – as probably the falling pigeon will do. This is just one of the incredible experiences that can happen during one's shooting days – mine started in 1891.

Yrs., EDWARD M. MILLAR,
Lynwood, Banchory,
Kincardineshire

ELEPHANT KILLED BY MOUSE

SIR, A MOST UNUSUAL AND probably unique experience with elephants has been reported by Captain F. Poppleton, a Park Warden of the Queen Elizabeth National Park in Uganda. He found the carcass of an elephant cow lying on her part-grown calf. An autopsy revealed a congestion of blood in the right lung and, in the middle of the congestion, was a tiny field-mouse which apparently had bolted up the cow's trunk, and she had burst a blood vessel while trying to cough it out again. When her strength gave out she collapsed upon the calf beside her, crushing the youngster to death.

Yrs., W. ROBERT FORAN
(Maj.), Nanyuki, Kenya

HOW A FOX GOT RID OF ITS FLEAS

SIR, WHILE DUCK SHOOTING a friend of mine saw bushes on one side of a pond shaking, and then from out of them came a fox carrying something white in its mouth. He entered the water backwards. Upon reaching the centre he very slowly sank out of sight, leaving the white object on the surface. Emerging from the opposite side, he shook himself vigorously and trotted off.

My friend's curiosity was roused and

procuring a long stick he drew the white object towards him; it was sheep's wool, and to his surprise was swarming with fleas!

Yrs., EDITH M. WEAVER,
Stoke Wood House, Limpley
Stoke, Bath

Sir, Mrs Weaver's story is not unique. Years ago my friend Cuthbert Binns saw precisely the same phenomenon. He saw a fox trot to the water's edge carrying, apparently, a tennis ball in his mouth. After some hesitation he walked into the water and very, very slowly immersed himself so that nothing but the tip of his nose with the tennis ball was visible above the water. In a few moments the fox was on the bank, having left the ball floating on the lake.

As in Mrs Weaver's story, the tennis ball turned out to be wool, which the fox must have laboriously collected from brambles and thickets; and, of course, it was teeming with fleas.

It was in Turkey – Asiatic Turkey – that Cuthbert Binns saw this strange performance. And not long before you had published a similar story from, I think, Scotland.

It is fascinating to conjecture how foxes in such distant places, separated by the North Sea, the whole of Europe and the Bosphorus, come to adopt the same ingenious method to rid themselves of fleas.

Yrs., J.W. SHEPHARD,
Glovers, Charlwood, Surrey

WELLINGTONS AND THE DUKE

Sir, In *THE FIELD* of 25 September it is said that the Iron Duke never wore rubber boots in his life, 'though he is always charged with having started the use of Wellingtons'.

The Wellingtons named after the Iron Duke were made of leather with soft morocco, or other thin skin, legs which reached half way up the shin bone underneath the cloth overall trousers. These trousers, which came into use about the time of the Peninsular War, fitted tightly round the instep and the heel of the boot and were strapped under the instep. These boots continued to be worn with military uniform up to the Second World War – both in leather for undress and in patent leather for mess dress – but I understand that the pattern has been somewhat altered.

The Wellington boot worn under the trousers has nothing to do with the rubber gumboot worn with trousers tucked inside it.

Yrs., 'SARTOR MILITARIS',
The Grove, Stocklynch,
Ilminster, Somerset

Sir, Your correspondent 'Sartor Militaris' is less than half right.

The footwear he describes is surely the half-Wellington. This was, until very recently, an article of naval uniform and was quite commonly worn in both day dress and mess dress, in its patent leather version.

I have always understood that the Wellington boot as worn by soldiers extended at least to the knee and generally above it, thus indicating how the rubber version came by its name.

> 'SARTOR NAVALIS', Junior
> Army and Navy Club,
> Horse Guards Avenue,
> London SW1

PHEASANT HITS GUN

Sir, WHEN SHOOTING WITH a neighbour last Thursday, 13 November, a curious incident happened to me. I was standing behind a wall and between two thorn bushes and beaters were advancing through a field of lucerne. A cock pheasant got up and flew straight and low towards me. It was too low to shoot at, and therefore, as it got close, I raised my gun, meaning to turn to shoot it after it had passed. However, the pheasant struck the muzzle of my gun and, as my fingers were probably on the trigger, the gun went off and the pheasant continued unhurt.

> Yrs., S.T. HOLLAND,
> Field Farm, Bibury, Gloucs.

FEARLESS FOXES

Sir, HAVING A CHILD TO tea one day in 1952, I produced my white polar teddy bear for her amusement, the bear's vintage was 1908, and was named Sir Ernest Shackleton. Guests having departed he was left sitting on the drawing room sofa. I came in from the garden at 8.30 pm and found a fox cub playing with him and, albeit a bit puzzled, trying to teach him to box. I did not even startle him so I left them to it and crept away. By 10 p.m. he had vanished. This was only 100 yards from the main road.

> Yrs., G.M.E. CHAMBERS,
> Sidelong Close, Lyme Regis,
> Dorset

1963

SHOOTING STICK PERILS

SIR, A SPORTING COUSIN AT the Cork Show had the misfortune to have his posterior penetrated by the shooting stick he was sitting on. Are such accidents frequent and what precautions can be taken against such a calamity?

Yrs., C. FURNESS,
Netherbyres, Eyemouth,
Berwickshire

[Not unprecedented nor, fortunately, frequent. Proper design renders it impossible. – Ed.]

DUEL IN THE SUN

SIR, I HAD AN EXPERIENCE with a Jordan valley shepherd in the troublesome 1930s which may be of interest. At that time, aircraft of 14 squadron used to fly low reconnaissance from Galilee to the Dead Sea and were often attacked *en passant* with slings and stones. We flew slowly, at about 80 knots, but the shepherds never learned to allow enough deflection, so we often saw the stone curving away astern. They were probably doing it more for fun than in anger, and we felt we should respond in kind. I therefore took off one day with the usual loaded guns and an egg.

Flying south at 20 ft., there appeared on the port bow a flock of goats and, sprinting to intercept my line of flight, the shepherd, a big, well-set man. As we passed about 25 yds. from him, he stopped, whirled his sling round his head and let go, and as usual missed behind.

I pulled up and came round at him in a dive as if to use the front gun, and remember clearly how he stood looking up at me, hesitant and undecided, unwilling to look for cover or to believe that I would really shoot. He looked as if he felt that the joke had gone far enough. I lobbed out an egg as in dive bombing and when I came round again it was clear from the way that he was laughing and waving that the egg must have burst pretty close to him.

So with mutual expressions of good will we parted. I wonder if David would have been quicker to judge the deflection if Goliath had given him a passing shot?

Yrs., T.C. TRAILL (Air Vice-Marshal), The Forge, Wilton, Marlborough

1964

THE VALE OF BEAVER

SIR,

Whene'er the Beaver leaves his cave
The river bank to scour,
We're right to speak its name as spelt,
And wrong to write 'Belvoir'!

Yet he who greets the Belvoir hounds
Is still a firm believer
That in this special case we must
Pronounce the name as 'Beaver'.

Can some kind reader of The Field
Explain why this should be?
As I can find no reason for
This strange anomaly.

Yrs., J.N.G.,
Harlow, Essex

SIR,

I cannot tell you why or how,
For nobody can know
A heifer should become a cow
And yet emit a low.

The vessel's front is called a bow,
The fiddle has a bow;
The bowsprit's rest is called a prow
The carrion bird's a crow

'Tis clear why old Laocoon
Is not pronounced lagoon,
But not why Scots have eaten scone
Ere kings were crowned at Scone.

Yrs., A.H. HASTIE,
Bury St Edmonds

SIR,

Living within its confines here
I've long been a believer
That they should spell it Belvedere
And then pronounce it Belvoir.

Yrs., H. T. MILNES,
Nether Broughton, Leics.

HEP CAT

SIR, I HAVE NEVER SEEN it definitely stated that the recent misbehaviour of 'Mods' and 'Rockers' can be traced to purple hearts and other drugs, now so regularly eaten by people of school age.

But I have a clue to this in the behaviour of an elderly cat who lives in this house and who, since being cured of a serious illness by means of pills and injections, has completely changed her character for the worse.

She now chases every animal within sight, yowls on the staircase most of the day when not engaged in bullying and frightening the life out of our other pets, and behaves exactly like those human counterparts of whom we read in the newspapers. She is perfectly well and runs like a pursued hare.

Yrs., E.H. WADE,
Bentley, Hampshire

1965

A SEAGULL PLOUGHED UNDER

SIR, WHEN PLOUGHING UP AN old grass field, our tractor drivers noticed that all the seagulls took flight and left the field. A few minutes later when passing the same spot one of them noticed a wing tip protruding from between the furrows.

He stopped his tractor and rescued a gull that had been ploughed under. The bird flew away apparently unhurt, but it was a long time before his pals plucked up enough courage to return.

It is a common and pretty sight to see gulls following the plough, but never before have I known one get close enough to be buried by the turning furrow.

Yrs., W.B. BROWN,
Winchester, Hants

SEEING THE SHOT

SIR, IN 1917, IN THE Ypres area, we were advancing in open order against a line of pillboxes and a strong point, Van Issaachar's Farm.

A rather heavy barrage was falling and one shell of large calibre, with flat trajectory, landed about 100 yds. directly in front of Lieut. Coley of the Royal Fusiliers.

It did not burst on impact but continued on at terrific speed, revolving fast and scattering mud and stones on either side.

Lieut. Coley *saw* it coming and, jumping high, let it pass between his legs, and it continued on far to the rear. The officer turned to me and said: 'Coo . . . I thought I saw my name on that one.'

Many lives were saved in this area by the soft and muddy nature of the ground which prevented these so-called 'dud shells' from exploding on impact.

Yrs., OLWEN P. ATTEWELL

1968

BUTTERFLIES

SIR, IT IS TWO YEARS since I wrote to you estimating that there were only about one fiftieth as many butterflies as there had been a decade earlier. Now butterflies are nearly completely absent and I fear this is the case over most of southern England. It is a disaster.

We have had many buddleia bushes spread over quite an area and not one single peacock or small tortoiseshell have I seen on them. The food of the caterpillars of these butterflies is nettles and these are abundant on this farm. A few years ago red admirals, painted ladies and common butterflies, too, could be seen here on any sunny day in July or August.

What has caused their disappearance and what can we do to prevent the extinction of one of the beauties of any garden? Accurate scientific information is necessary, backing co-ordinated co-operation on a wide scale for a long period. Where is this available and who can guide the work?

Yrs., O.H.M. HERFORD,
Hawkhurst, Herefordshire

Sir, This seems to be an exceptionally good year for peacock butterflies.

On 23 August, the second day of a sunny spell, the average of several counts showed there were about 59 peacocks on our one buddleia bush, as well as a handful of 'whites', a tortoiseshell and a small copper, with many bumble and honey bees.

In other parts of the garden, at the same time, peacocks predominated over all other butterflies.

Yrs., JOAN BRUCE,
Hemel Hempstead, Herefordshire

Sir, This year in the garden we have an unusually large number of the small tortoiseshell butterflies. I have counted 40 on one buddleia bush this weekend.

On 9 September, in warm sunshine, I noted on the buddleia bushes dozens of tortoiseshells, a red admiral, three or four peacocks, a comma and the brimstone.

Earlier this month we had two painted ladies. There have also been the wall brown, a ringlet or two and the holly blue.

Yrs., W.S. BISHOP,
Purley, Surrey

A DOG'S TRAFFIC SENSE

Sir, A few weeks ago I was in a taxi travelling down Piccadilly towards Knightsbridge when the taxi driver stopped suddenly at a pedestrian crossing by Green Park. He jumped out, held up the dense traffic in both directions and escorted a rather elderly mongrel across the road. He said he knew the dog well. It always waited there for someone to take it across, but where it went to after that, he was unable to discover.

Yrs., J.N. NEWGASS (Mrs),
Dorchester, Dorset

A hunt terrier which had been hit by a car. He broke one hind leg and dislocated the other. He developed strong shoulder muscles and walked on two legs while his injuries healed. He now walks on all four.

Sir, Mrs Newgass's letter can be confirmed by an incident which I saw one evening last month. Walking along the north side of Piccadilly, opposite Green Park, I noticed an off-white creature of dubious parentage inspecting the passers-by – all this within rifle shot of the Kennel Club.

He cast a baleful eye over me and wandered off. However, when I turned to cross at a pedestrian crossing, he appeared from nowhere and fell in correctly on my left side, nose level with my knee.

We got half-way across to the safety of the island, past which swept a stream of crazed commuters. Minutes later the chance came and we crossed to the park.

Inside, my companion accelerated and in a matter of seconds was making particularly rude advances to a female dog of French origin taking its constitutional on the end of a lead held by an elderly lady.

She looked round in dismay, making ineffectual shooing noises. I hurried past, averting my gaze, but not before the mongrel, I swear, glanced at me and winked.

Yrs., GEOFFREY ARMITAGE,
Owermoigne, Dorset

Sir, Mrs Newgass appears to be referring to Percy, though the description of him as a 'rather elderly mongrel' is unflattering. He lives at 107b Piccadilly and commutes between there and Green Park.

Yrs., J.W. STEWART,
London SW1

1970

HOOVES OUT OF LINE

SIR, DURING THE MASTERSHIP of the late John Watson, the Meath Hunt acquired the distinction of being known as the Premier Pack.

During this period, the Empress Eugenie of Austria and her household hunted from Summerhill House, and my father was present when one of the party, a princeling or archduke, riding a young blood horse, had the misfortune to kick a hound within sight of the Master.

The unfortunate Nimrod was duly castigated before an enormous field and finally, in stentorian voice, ordered to go home, following which the tirade was taken over by the Master's wife, who continued to harangue until they were out of sight. Those were the days.

Yrs., A.L. LOWRY,
Navan, Co. Meath

THE FOXHUNTING DUKE

SIR, HAVING READ MISS MCCRAITH'S admirable letter about HRH The Duke of Windsor as a foxhunter in Leicestershire in 1921 and 1922, I hasten to endorse everything she says. He was certainly not a bad horseman. He was always faultlessly turned out, with his slim figure and good legs for a boot, showing not only himself but horses that he rode, to advantage.

He went like the wind. When he had falls it was because he liked riding 'chasers and point-to-pointers and to take the Quorn and the Cottesmore fences fast with a forward seat and riding short. His falls were due to his horses stumbling or pecking or falling on landing.

Colonel George Drummond was supposed to give him the lead and on several occasions George Drummond, who had a pretty strong temper, expostulated with HRH when he found him not following but jumping fences in the first flight, yards away on his (Drummond's) off or near flank. It would go like this: 'Sire, I am supposed to give you a lead; if you break your neck it will not be my fault but I will always get the blame.'

As Miss McCraith says, there were so many famous first-flighters of both sexes in those days who are now dead. They knew almost every acre of land, all the coverts and generally the line that a fox would

take. Happily I am still alive to add to her memories, as are several more who, I am sure, will agree.

At that time I was living and hunting in the Belvoir country and writing the Hunt's doings for the *Daily Telegraph*, which helped to buy oats for my two horses. But I was superbly mounted one day a week with the Quorn and the Cottesmore by generous friends who had hunters to spare, which enabled me sometimes to live in a run with the 'Cut 'em down and hang 'em out to dry' thrusters.

Yrs., SCARSDALE,
Kedleston, Derby

Sir, The remark quoted from George Drummond's diary, 'He was naturally unfit', surprised me. He was one of the fittest men I ever came across.

I remember the hunt referred to from Greens Norton. I was Master of the Grafton at the time and the meet was at my house. It was a great hunt and not many saw the end of it. Just as hounds were running into Bucknalls they checked in a lane and the Duke jumped into the middle of them. I said, 'Oh Sir, Sir,' he turned round, jumped out of the lane and coming up to me said, 'So sorry, but it was not an occasion for "Sir, Sir". Where the hell are you going you so and so would have been more appropriate.'

We had another good hunt early that same afternoon – and I suggested we had had about enough and should take the hounds home. The Duke said, 'Isn't it a pity to waste such a good scenting day, there's plenty of light for another draw?' So we drew again and had another good 20 minutes. Not many took part in it as most men and horses had had enough.

On the way home I asked the Duke if he would come in and have a cup of tea. He replied, 'No thanks very much, I have a big official dinner this evening and I want to get back to London to have time for a game of squash before going to it.'

On another day hacking through Wappenham village on the way to draw he asked me if there was any old or sick person who he could help by going to see. On being told of a bed-ridden old body who had always been a great supporter of fox-hunting, he went to his cottage and had a chat with him. It is actions of that sort that have made our Royal Family so popular.

The Duke, the late King and Prince Henry were all first rate men to hounds and thoroughly enjoyed their hunting. I remember on one occasion Prince Henry jumping into a field of wheat and being cursed by the irate owner.

He apologized most humbly to the farmer and to me and said, 'Promise me you'll never tell him who it was he cursed. I thoroughly deserved it but it might embarrass him if he knew who it was that he had cursed in front of the whole field.'

Yrs., V.D.S. WILLIAMS,
Farnham Royal, Bucks.

PEPPERING AN UNCLE

SIR, MY FATHER HAD a great friend, a gentleman of distinction who was not known to be safe with a gun, particularly when shooting grouse. One day whilst walking up grouse in Perthshire, a shot rang out and I saw my uncle roll over like a shot rabbit and then lie motionless.

I rushed to him to find out what had happened. He had certainly been peppered but in that part of the anatomy which is most suited to absorb pellets. I told him he had given me an awful fright and asked him why he had lain so still. 'To avoid the second barrel,' he replied.

Yrs., R.G. POLLOK-McCALL
(Maj.), Ross and Cromarty

ONE-UP FOR A WOODPECKER

SIR, EACH SPRING WE are visited by a spotted woodpecker who drums on our television aerial, making a noise resembling a road drill and shattering the silence of the woodlands. For the amusement of our startled visitors we offer one of two explanations: That he is mentally retarded and has not learnt in four seasons that there are no bugs in the metal-work; or that he is playing one-upmanship over the others who can drum only on our pine trees.

Yrs., BARBARA CLEMENT,
(The Head Deaconess of the
Central House of the Deaconess
Order), Hindhead, Surrey

A SQUIRREL ATTACKS A DOG

SIR, A FEW YEARS AGO while out shooting a squirrel jumped from a tree on to the neck of my dog, where it took a firm hold with claws and teeth. There was much howling from the dog until I managed to detach the squirrel from the dog with the aid of my stick – not wishing to sacrifice my hands. There was no reason for this vicious attack for the squirrel was out of danger in the top of a tree and was unnoticed by the dog until the attack.

Yrs., C.M.D. SANKEY
Wolverhampton, Staffs.

Sir, My Irish Wolfhound is always keen to chase that which moves, and has often been bemused by a squirrel's apparent disappearance (up a tree).

In late October last year, my hound seemed to have his way when he met a squirrel about 50 yards from a tree. The squirrel turned and faced my hound who, surprised by this, skidded to a halt and approached cautiously. When close enough the squirrel darted forward and delivered two blows to the hound's nose. One drew blood. The squirrel then ran back to the clump of trees he started from. The hound did not seem to be bothered by this and he has chased a few squirrels since.

Yrs., K. FOLLETT,
Banstead, Surrey

1971

A GROUSE IN THE HAT

SIR, WHILE SHOOTING IN the afternoon butts on the home beat at Farleyer on Saturday, 21 August, Mr Charles Smithgall, a visitor from Gainsville, Georgia, marked down a lightly wounded bird that pitched 100 yards behind his butt.

At the end of the drive when dogs were despatched to recover it, it took to the wing and made a low pass over Mr Smithgall's position.

The drive being over and his guns being unloaded, Mr Smithgall could only vent his spleen by removing his hat and waving it. The bird flew into the hat, which happily had a tall crown.

After a short scuffle, during which Mr Smithgall was seen to dive into the heather as if touching down a try, he despatched the bird by *coup de main*. This all goes to show that a bird in the hat is worth several on the wing.

Yrs., NEIL RAMSAY,
Aberfeldy, Perthshire

PARTRIDGE STOPS CAR

SIR, THIS LITTLE STORY is almost unbelievable. We were off to a cocktail party one lovely evening last spring, at a friend's house in the county of Wiltshire (where we were living at the time), motoring by quiet lanes, keeping away from the main roads, which is always our habit.

On rounding a bend in the road, suddenly a largish bird flew straight towards us, as if to come through the windscreen. We slowed down automatically. The bird flew round and dived at us again from the right-hand side. I then saw that it was a partridge. We stopped the car, as the bird seemed to be attacking us for some reason.

I noticed what I thought to be some horse droppings right in the middle of the empty road some distance away. The partridge flew down to these droppings. Spreading her wings, she fluttered on to them, and to our amazement they were young chicks.

They all got up and she ushered them very slowly over the road.

Yrs., WINNIE ASPINAL,
Axminster, Devon

A STAG FROM THE SEA

SIR, APROPOS AMPHIBIOUS animals, in the early 1920s the Mid-Kent released their carted stag from just south of Hothfield one morning. The stag took the hounds to Dymchurch and also took to the sea where the pack was called off.

The stag, Charley, judging tide and current correctly, turned east towards Sandgate, where it made a safe landing.

On emerging, the animal was viewed by a character well known for his lengthy midday sessions at a local pub, who, on seeing this monster with horns, protruding eyes and nostrils, which seemed to breathe fire, ran screaming down the esplanade shouting:

'Everyone stay indoors! The devil himself has landed from France!' He locked himself in his house and was said never to have touched a drink again.

Meanwhile the hunt staff had arrived with a horse box, and on one of the whips saying gently, 'Come on, Charley, hunting's over for today,' the animal shook himself once and stepped delicately up the ramp into the box and so back to kennels to enjoy a hearty supper and many further hunts.

Yrs., ARTHUR WELLESLEY
(Maj.), London SW3

1972

HARE ON A SWAN'S BACK

Sir, While walking through a small spinney at the end of which was a wide stream, a fully grown brown hare got up and ran to cross the stream. At the same time a swan was swimming along the stream and the hare, in order to escape, jumped on the back of the swan and from there to the bank.

This was witnessed by several people on the far side of the bank.

Yrs., MICHAEL PELLY,
Sonning Common, Berks.

OTTERHOUNDS TO MINK

Sir, It is almost a truism to state that there are too few otters and too many mink at large.

Might it be possible for otterhounds to give chase to mink? If this feat of venery could be achieved, the otterhounds could become the heroes of rural England.

I know too little of hounds to be able to assess if they would like this idea, but how marvellous if they did!

Yrs., AUBERON HERBERT,
Dulverton, Somerset

WILD DAFFODILS

Sir, From time to time we hear from non-hunting people tales of the damage done to growing crops and plants and I have always been inclined to write them

off, without possessing any actual evidence.

But on 20 March, after the Ledbury Foxhounds had met at Dymock, I was able to see just what happens to tender growth when fox and hounds run through it.

The woods around Dymock and Much Marcle (on the Gloucestershire/Herefordshire border) are beautifully carpeted with an almost continuous covering of wild daffodils and on this date the blooms were just at their best with their dainty and frail stalks and their charming tiny yellow trumpets.

Three times during the day I saw the hunted fox, followed by 20 couple of hounds, run at a real pace through the flowers and yet, after they had gone, scarcely a single bloom had been damaged.

How is it that animals can be so neat when the trail of only a couple of human beings is that of ugly destruction?

Yrs., 'LOPPYLUGS',
Bromsgrove, Worcs.

STOAT AND EGG

SIR, I WAS DRIVING BACK to Hermitage along the country lanes leading to Yattendon when I saw the most extraordinary sight of an egg, and it looked like a peewit's egg, being trundled across the road by a stoat.

It was pushing with its nose and front feet and, as I approached it, somewhat fast over a knoll of a hill, it bolted back, leaving the egg in the middle of the road.

I have seen rats move hen's eggs, but I have never before seen a stoat move an egg. Has anyone else?

Yrs., JACK HATT,
Goring Heath, Berks.

Sir, The following incident, which I saw some years ago while fishing on the River Meon, between Droxford and Soberton, will, I think, interest Mr Hatt.

I was watching the head of a pool, where a carrier emerged from a swamp of high rushes to join the main stream on the left bank.

A stoat appeared from the mouth of the carrier carrying a moorhen's egg and swam across the pool to the right bank.

My impression was that the rounded end of the egg was under the chin and the pointed end pressed into the base of the neck between the throat and the top of the chest.

The stoat appeared to have no difficulty in swimming, although the head was held high with the pole slightly arched; nor did it have an apparent difficulty leaving the water on the right bank.

As far as I could see it did not stop on landing or make any adjustment to the position of the egg, but disappeared into the long grass heading for the hedge and bank at the side of the lane, which, at this point ran parallel to the stream about 10 yards away.

Yrs., E.C.L. DAY,
Winchester, Hants

A CAT AGAINST THE ODDS

SIR, AREN'T CATS BRAVE? Ours, who is about 1.1 hh at the withers, was crouching over her supper saucer when our Borzoi craned down to see what he could have. What he got was a couple of lightning swift slashes across his aristocratic nose. He withdrew, baffled.

Sir, if a man 35 ft. tall and about 250 in. round the chest, leaned over while you were dining, would you punch him on the nose?

Yrs., J.D. WILSON,
Landford Wood, Wilts.

SQUIRREL SWIMS THE SPEY

SIR, FISHING ON THE Spey in July, I was wading down a pool when I felt a movement at my back.

Thinking that my wading staff had turned with the current I reached out to free it. To my astonishment an animal was trying to climb up. At first I thought it was a water-rat, but it was a red squirrel.

It managed to clamber up to my shoulder but I was able to get a grip behind its neck.

After a tugging match, I dislodged it.

It swam off over the strong current and landed on a rock on the other side, shook itself and glowered at me, obviously thinking what a peculiar tree he had tried to rest on. After a pause he disappeared.

Yrs., C.M. SHANKLAND,
Walton-on-Thames

RAW KIDNEY

SIR, I WENT OUT STALKING recently with a guest at our lodge. We shot a stag at 12.45 and, after 'gralloching' it, we dragged it a short way before stopping for lunch.

During lunch I was surprised to see this man cut one of the kidneys out of the carcass and eat it raw. I have never seen this done before.

Yrs., A.L. JOHNSON,
Broadford, Isle of Skye

Sir, With reference to 'Raw Kidney', I, too, have had a similar experience.

Some years ago two of us shot four wild goats in Kirkcudbrightshire for dog food. On returning to my car, having dragged the goats off the hill, I was startled to see that my companion appeared to be bleeding from the mouth. I asked him if he was all right and his nonchalant reply, followed by a large bite from a gory mass in his hand, effectively calmed my fears for his well-being, and routed me to the privacy of some bracken to decant my lunch.

He had, it transpired, been lunching nearby off the warm kidneys of a particularly pungent billy-goat. He was not a tall man and I have always suspected that his ancestry must have included a line of pigmy head-hunters!

Yrs., A.J. RANKEN,
Fordingbridge, Hants

1973

THE SPIRIT OF FOXHUNTING

SIR, I AM WRITING TO relate an incident that happened out hunting this season in north Yorkshire, as I feel it shows the true spirit of hunting and the sportsman's attitude to the quarry.

The incident happened when the lady secretary of the hunt was following in her car and came upon the hunted fox caught fast in barbed wire trying to get through a hedge on to the road. It was so tangled it would have been impossible to free itself, so the lady, with great daring, untangled

the fox, who did not take long to put a good distance between himself and his rescuer.

I believe we who hunt enjoy it because we admire and respect old Charlie and take our hats off to him and hope he will be able to run free in this over-human-populated island of ours for many hundreds of years to come. Wildlife will be preserved as long as we have our field sports.

Yrs., PEGGY ALEXANDER,
Appleton Wiske, Yorkshire

PHEASANTS: FEWER GUNS

SIR, THERE HAVE BEEN TOO many unsavoury stories in recent years in connection with the slaughter of huge numbers of low pheasants. Although these excesses are certainly the exception rather than the rule, they do untold harm to shooting in general.

I have always maintained that it is virtually impossible to shoot more than about 350 really good pheasants in a day. With low pheasants the limit is probably in the region of 3,000 these days, although the Edwardians managed up to 4,000 occasionally.

I have often heard people tell of a superb day of 600 or more very high pheasants. Upon investigation I have invariably found that there was one or possibly two drives of very good birds and the day is remembered for those birds. The 400 or so indifferent pheasants that were shot at the remaining drives are conveniently forgotten.

Where it is virtually impossible to make pheasants fly really well I see nothing wrong in shooting 500/600 on the bigger days, particularly if this can be done late in the season. The number of shots fired will probably be much the same as on the 300-day of much more difficult pheasants.

In both cases it is important that everyone has plenty to shoot at. However in that context I do think that 1,000 pheasants in a day is too many and 2,000 is revolting.

In a further effort to improve the quality of the sport in the future may I also suggest that eight guns is usually too many. In my experience it is impossible to put pheasants over a front of eight guns unless those guns are much too close, which is all too often the case. Less pheasants and better pheasants but let us do it with six guns and dogs by invitation.

Yrs., C.P. HAZLEHURST,
Broomy Court, Llandinabo,
Herefordshire

1974

PINK COAT

SIR, A HUNTING COAT OF any colour, black, red, or green, could quite correctly be called a Pink coat. The word Pink had nothing to do with the colour but was the name of a well-known and exclusive firm of tailors who specialised in hunting clothes.

Yrs., JOHN BOWERMAN,
The Manor, Pewsey, Wilts.

COW AND BALL

SIR, WHEN I WAS A midshipman in HMS *Bellerophon* in the spring of 1912, we were lying in Bantry Bay, south-west Ireland, and two of us went ashore to play golf on the local rough but intriguing course. It was a needle match, my honour at the longest hole on the course. I drove a straight but short ball. My opponent hit a poor sliced drive, his ball landing close to a cow, who, somewhat surprised, picked it up in her mouth; whereupon my wily Irish opponent rushed upon the, by now, startled creature and drove her towards the hole until just short of the green, when he made her disgorge the ball, which was quite undamaged. So my opponent had 'driven' well over 400 yards and with two putts achieved what might have been called a 'cowie'.

Yrs., E.L. TOMKINSON,
Egerton, nr. Ashford, Kent

THE BAD IN A BLADE

SIR, A FEW MONTHS AGO I provided my gardener with a new blade for his scythe. I was somewhat surprised when, in the course of a conversation with him, he asked me if I would take the blade into town to have it 'set' to the shaft.

[193]

On inquiring why there had been such a delay, he told me that he had been leaving the blade out in the open 'to get the bad out of it'. Further questioning led him to tell me that one should always rust a blade 'to get the bad out'.

Apparently, the best method, in days gone by, was to leave a blade for a month in pig-wash, the sourer the pig-wash the better. Is this a common practice throughout the country and are there any similar practices?

Yrs., J.F. KENYON,
Pradoe, Oswestry, Salop

Sir, With reference to the letter on scythe blades, I have heard of brushing hooks being left to rust for a time before use.

When I first started using a scythe I was told that the blade must always be sharpened at the end of the day's work. This was to prevent the devil playing with it and ruining the blade. If it was sharp, he would cut his fingers and leave it alone. Also, I was once told that it was permissible for farmworkers to cut 'sneads', or scythe handles, on anyone's land.

Yrs., DAVID WILLIAMS,
Maesbury, Oswestry, Salop

Albino swallows perch side by side at a Yorkshire farm near Driffield, East Riding. They were hatched from a nest in an outbuilding but, since their departure in 1969, have not been seen again.

Sir, I read the letter about the bad in the blade. I have been a slaughterman for about 40 years and what is said is the truth.

We in the trade know that if a knife is rubbed and one tries to use it the same day it is useless. I was given a knife about 10 years ago. It was an English brand (Gregory), which usually we would not use, because the American knife (Green River brand) was better.

The Gregory knife, which was 50 years old and had been little used, turned out to be the best knife I ever had. Also, a butcher's steel left in the ground for a number of years is the same.

> Yrs., HAROLD WALSH,
> 99 Stonyhurst Road, Blackburn,
> Lancs.

Sir, My grandfather was a journeyman blacksmith and also a tenant of a small farm in north-east Cheshire in the early 1900s. He was, so I understand, an expert user of the scythe and on one occasion cut a swathe 140 yards long of meadow grass, without using a whetstone.

After hay time he would detach the blade from the pole and place the former on the roof of an outbuilding which had a stone flagged surface. It remained there until the following June when it was attached to the pole again. I can only assume that this 'weathering' improved the steel's ability to retain a keen cutting edge.

> Yrs., J.M. HOWARD,
> Torkington, Hazel Grove,
> nr. Stockport

1977

MUSIC OF THE HUNT

SIR, THE ANSWER TO YOUR article 'Has Modern Foxhunting Gone Quiet?', is most definitely yes, with the passing of professional huntsmen like Jim Welsh and the Thatchers.

That beautiful sound and music one heard from these men is missing from some hunts today. What a thrill one received from the sound of these men if Reynard decided to go twice round the rookery before breaking cover. The view halloo coupled with the horn blowing was magic, with fields of a thousand followers, including the Duke of Windsor and his brothers, after the hunt ball in Oakham was an experience never to be forgotten.

I was a second horseman with the Cottesmore and Belvoir and now occasionally follow a hunt where the horn blowing and view halloos are out at the Master's request – pity. No disrespect to these gentlemen without whom many packs would fold-up.

Yrs., ALFRED DUFFILL,
12 Thrushcraig Cres., Paisley

OTTER ON SALMON FLY

SIR, IN THE EASTER holidays I was fishing with my father on Loch Beg on the river Thurso when he hooked, played and landed a partially grown otter on a large garry tubefly.

The otter took the fly with a perfect head and tail rise and was in no way foul hooked. It played like a small salmon, making several strong runs but on being brought to the bank it promptly beached itself by walking up it.

We debated with our ghillie, Alister, how best to rid it of the fly and decided to try giving it slack line. This my father did three times; the first it walked further up the bank, the second it took another swim in the loch, but the third time it sat close to us on the bank, and scrabbling with its front paws at the fly, managed to get it out.

So ended in the happiest possible way a most unusual incident. It would be interesting to hear if any other readers have had a similar experience.

Yrs., SIMON I. McKAY,
Winder House, Sedbergh School,
Cumbria

HOW A WOODCOCK DOES IT

SIR, ALTHOUGH THE carrying of its young by a woodcock is well documented, I feel the incidence is similar to seeing ghosts. Until one has seen a ghost, one is sceptical.

In the early morning of 23 April, I was driving along a track in mixed woodland on our shoot. On rounding a bend, a woodcock and fully fledged chick were present in the middle of the track, approximately 10 yards from the car.

The chick crouched but the parent ran off a few feet, stopped, and then returned to the chick circling it twice. It then mounted the chick from behind and with laboured flight, its wings actually hitting the ground, it lifted the young bird and flew about 10 yards before crash-landing in a clearing. Both birds then ran into the undergrowth. The legs of the young bird were obvious below the parent in flight, but I could not see the legs of the adult so presume they were tucked up to support its young. I have now seen my ghost.

Yrs., A.B.L. PEAKE,
Hampstead Norryes, Newbury,
Berks.

1980

TICKLING FOR TROUBLE

Sir, I spent one day last week on the high ground at Bloodylaws studying curlew, plover, redshank and snipe. I had to heel my labrador and springer. I rested by a burn and seeing some tiny trout frantically dashing about an equally tiny pool I decided to attempt to touch a trout and recapture an excitement of youth.

Lying on the bank I reached into a hole where I had seen some fish taking refuge. The depth was greater than I anticipated and with the water to the top of my arm I got a 'feel'.

The round belly was big, which surprised me. I would not have thought such a large fish would be living in such a small burn. To get a proper grip I fingered along the body and was surprised to touch a pair of legs. Thinking I had a horny toad I decided to retrieve it for study but I was seized by a set of very sharp teeth and withdrew my hand in horror. Clasped to my left index finger was a large rat.

In the confusion that followed my springer despatched the offending beast. This rat had probably had a rich diet of moorland birds' eggs and so we are well rid of him.

In any event the only concern I felt was for myself. My finger was oozing blood and fearing some 'dreaded lurgy' I quickly made my way home for wifely attention.

So gentlemen, if you have a notion as I had, take great care.

Yrs., MARTIN NAUGHTON,
Jedburgh, Roxburghshire

SHOOTING CHECKLIST

Sir, Mr Duncan Robertson's idea of a checklist for shooting is most sensible. My own is a little larger and consists of the following items: Husky jacket, spare Husky jacket, deer stalker, guns, gun slips, cartridges, cartridge belt, number draw, card and pencil, gumboots and spare pair, gumboot socks and spare pair, gumboot remover, stick (not shooting stick), dog lead and whistle, priest.

Waterproof bag containing: ear plugs and spare pair, mittens and spare pair, spare deer stalker, small binoculars, shotproof spectacles, cartridge extractor, headache pills, face mask for pigeon shooting, bar of chocolate, packet of boiled sweets,

band-aid, Barbour jacket, one apple, mackintosh trousers, spare pair mackintosh
trousers, butt marker, left hand glove and
spare, camera and spare film, spare handkerchief, knife, box of matches, veterinary
wound powder, pair boot laces and univer-
sal plug for wash basin/bath (useful when
shooting abroad).

I may look like a Christmas tree, but it is
amazing how often I am able to provide an
item of equipment or clothing for a fellow
gun.

Yrs., RICHARD
GREENWOOD,
Balcombe, Sussex

1981

LEAPING SALMON

SIR, IN 1951, ON Loch Clachan, a salmon of 13 lb., immediately on being hooked in very rough water, charged the boat and jumped in, causing a very unseemly scramble by the ghillie and myself, which would have done credit to any international rugger match! On the same Loch, I also saw a fish hooked, jump and land on the thwart and then jump out again, unfortunately breaking the cast in the process, and the same thing happened to me subsequently.

I know from personal knowledge that on the Grimersta, Brigadier General Weston some years ago, while playing a salmon, had another salmon following it, leap into the boat, at the same time he was landing a fish, and a similar thing happened to Vice-Admiral, the Honourable Rupert Drummond on the Blackwater. All these instances took place in the 1950s.

It may also interest readers to know that on Loch Clachan I twice had two salmon on the same cast, but on both occasions I only succeeded in landing the one on the dropper, but the way the water exploded when two salmon about 10 lb. both seized the flies on the dropper and the tail at the same time, I am not likely to forget, quite apart from the drenching I received.

Yrs., K.G.P. MACKENZIE,
Chittlehampton, Devon

1982

THE COUNTRYMAN

SIR, DURING A RECENT conversation with an old friend the term 'a real countryman' was used. 'How do you define that expression?' I asked, and 'How will I know this real countryman when I meet him?' The reply I received was as follows:

He will never fail to pick up a piece of wire, an old bottle, an old tin and even a piece of plastic baler twine and carry it to somewhere safe and put it where he can make sure no stock can come to any harm from it.

He will always be counting things: he never says 'I have just seen a good covey of partridges' but will say 'I have seen a good covey of 12 partridges' or whatever. He will never say 'I see George X has got a nice bunch of black Hereford bullocks in his front field' but will always say how many.

He usually walks with a stick, generally a fairly long one, and will always knock over a thistle as he passes it.

He will always refer to trees by their proper names and he will always know 'which way the wind blows'.

I wonder if any of your readers would agree.

Yrs., C.H. COATES,
Billesley, Warwicks.

1983

CUCKOO SONG

Sir, Recently, while reading about the habits of the cuckoo I remembered an incident which took place two years ago.

During the late part of May, or possibly early June 1981, I witnessed a most unusual occurrence. A pair of cuckoos, whether male and female I am not certain, alighted together on an overhead cable just beyond the perimeter of my garden.

The pair began to call out their enchanting song, and I had been watching for approximately half a minute when suddenly their individual calls began to register in perfect unison. This lasted for about 15 seconds.

Yrs., R. CARTER-JONES,
Yafford, Isle of Wight

Sir, I was interested to read the letter from Mr R. Carter-Jones describing how he heard two cuckoos singing in unison. I had a similar experience early one June morning last summer while cycling near Shipston-on-Stour. But whereas my two cuckoos were in perfect unison as regards time, one was slightly sharper than the other in pitch. The effect was most unusual.

Incidentally Mr Carter-Jones' two cuckoos must both have been males. The female cuckoo does not utter the familiar cuckoo call. Her song is a liquid bubbling sound.

Yrs., LEO DUNHAM,
Oundle, Northants.

1984

EGG THIEVES

SIR, I HAND-REARED A bitch stoat, which lived in the house for two years and she was passionately fond of eggs. She found it impossible to pierce the shells of sound eggs with her teeth for the simple reason that the radius of the shell, even on eggs as small as pigeon or partridge, was so large and the shell so smooth, that her teeth slid off without damaging the surface.

This did not prevent her eating eggs. In her frustrated effort to bite them, she pushed them around by her nose, as circus dogs play 'football' until, sooner or later, the egg collided with something solid enough to shatter the shell. This was not a deliberate, intelligent act but the result of random efforts to bite her prey.

When the shell shattered, she ate the contents and it was at this time, when the shell was broken, that she pierced it with her teeth. The punctures might have fitted the stoat skulls Mr Gill keeps in his laboratory – but they do not prove that they were made by a stoat in an undamaged egg.

Another old wives' tale is that a super rat, with an IQ up to Mensa standard, will steal an egg, clutch it in all four legs and roll on his back. A ratty assistant will then clutch his tail and tow rat and egg safely home.

I confess that even if I saw a rat with my own eyes, clutching an unbroken egg, and another rat apparently towing him home, I should suspect that they were either quarrelling over it – or that it was time to take my cue to smell a rat.

> Yrs., PHIL DRABBLE,
> Abbots Bromley, Staffs.

Sir, It is not an old wives' tale that a rat will lay on his back clutching an egg with his legs while other rats drag him away by his tail. A good many years ago we kept hens in some old stabling and I knew rats were taking their eggs.

One day, I went in with a stick to see two rats dragging a third rat by its tail. This rat was holding an egg between his four legs. The towing rats were very quick off the mark and escaped but the towed rat was too slow and met his Waterloo. The egg also perished.

> Yrs., H.B. CRANE (Capt.),
> 36 Orchard Drive, Wye, Kent

Sir, Whilst not wishing to question the accuracy of Captain Crane's observation, I do wonder at his interpretation of their motives.

Most folk tales originate from accurate observation, muddled by anthropomorphic matching animal instinct to human intelligence.

Rats are quarrelsome creatures, far more

likely to steal each other's food than to help secrete it.

My guess is that the Captain witnessed one thief being mugged by two others. Ascribing such altruistic motives to their felony persuades me to join Mr Drabble in smelling a rat.

Yrs., J. FLANNAGAN,
The Hollies, Stratford Road,
Hall Green

1990

AQUATIC PHEASANT CHICK

SIR, OVER THE PAST few days, a hen pheasant with a brace of chicks at foot has been foraging intermittently amid the stones on the partly exposed bed of the river Barle, 150 yards downstream of Dulverton bridge. Occasionally she flies across the twenty yards of water from one bank to another, presumably having instructed her young to lie low in the undergrowth on the bank during her absence. I have just seen one of the chicks, roughly a week old, break cover and swim across the river after its mother.

It seemed to swim just as effectively as the mallard ducklings which infest this stretch of river. Is this a common practice of baby pheasants?

The occurrence was also seen by a Jesuit priest, surely not far behind a Commissioner of Oaths as a witness of quality.

Yrs., JAMES IRVINE
ROBERTSON,
Dulverton, Somerset

INDEX